THIS
MUST
BE
THE
PLACE

THIS MUST BE THE PLACE

How Music Can Make Your City Better

Shain Shapiro

Repeater

Published by Repeater Books

An imprint of Watkins Media Ltd

Unit 11 Shepperton House

89-93 Shepperton Road

London

N1 3DF

United Kingdom

www.repeaterbooks.com

A Repeater Books paperback original 2023

1

Distributed in the United States by Random House, Inc., New York.

Copyright Shain Shapiro © 2023

Shain Shapiro asserts the moral right to be identified as the author of this work.

ISBN: 9781915672056

Ebook ISBN: 9781915672063

Printed and bound in the United Kingdom by TJ Books Limited

For Alli

CONTENTS

PROLOGUE
WHY MUSIC MATTERS

This book is my attempt to honour my love of music by exploring its impact on how we live, and how it shapes the places we call home. I'll show the effect music has on how cities are developed, built, managed and governed. We all live in an ecosystem and music is a subsection of that — an ecosystem within an ecosystem — and if we understand what it is and how it relates to us and our built environment, we can use it to make places better — and we all benefit.

Music is many things. It is the industry that makes, manufactures and distributes art as a product. It is part of our education curriculum. It is a mental and social wellbeing tool. It is widely available yet innately inequitable. Where you live, what you look like and what music you make systemically impacts your ability to sell it and earn a living. It is also a way for understanding not only why places become vibrant and succeed, but also why they are inequitable and fail. We can point to how certain cities reap economic investment from music, while others fail to maximise its benefits.

Music is something we all share in celebration. We sing "Happy Birthday" to each other, we attend concerts and festivals to relax and have fun, we strum on a guitar and prod a piano to relieve stress, we sing in choirs. When a crisis hits, many of these acts become a source of comfort or salvation — our balconies become stages, webcams facilitate choirs. Music becomes a source of conviviality and community-building, a framework to keep us together when we're forced to be apart, but the process that leads to these things happening is not protected nor equitably managed, and when festivals and concerts are cancelled, youth groups and libraries shut, and music gatherings are effectively banned, as in the first few waves of the COVID-19 pandemic, the expansive economic and cultural foundation that these activities underpin collapses. Jobs are lost. Mental health suffers. Music has never been under threat, but what gets it to us — the jobs, supply chain and skills — is.

The challenges facing the music sector due to the fallout of the pandemic — which I'll cover later — have also highlighted the challenges embedded in policy-making. Little urgency was placed on protecting jobs in the music business because music remained available through streaming services, on YouTube, on our smartphones and televisions. Just like any other form of infrastructure, music touches all of us, whether we recognise it or not. Similar to private companies bottling tap water and selling it as purified water, music starts as a public good — singing nursery rhymes, lullabies, learning an instrument in school — and then becomes owned, ordered, managed and distributed privately. We all deserve access to music, but in many places this is not the case.

Music has different meanings for all of us, but no matter who we are or where we live, we can all be engaged in and work to create more resilient music ecosystems that make all our places better. What is missing, and what this book offers, is a toolkit of policies, frameworks and examples of how people, organisations and initiatives around the world are engaging with, measuring and bettering their music ecosystems. From the work that I have done with my firm Sound Diplomacy, to artist-led protests in Melbourne, to government fostering much-needed dialogue in London, to a consortium of public and private sector partners in

Huntsville, Alabama, music has proven to grow economies, bring people closer together and make places better. But this requires a deliberate and intentional approach, which I have been developing for over a decade and continue to refine and learn from every day. Better understanding the role of music in who we are, where we live, how we interact and why we invest in what we do reveals a story about all of us. And this story is explained through my experiences working to develop music policy in London, Madison, Wisconsin, Huntsville, Alabama and other places, while also chronicling the efforts of others, from Melbourne to Sydney, Austin to Nashville.

All of these stories begin with someone, somewhere, deciding that not only was music important to them, but they could see that by improving the circumstances and policies around it, their community as a whole would improve. All these lessons began with on-the-ground grassroots challenges — a venue closing down or frustrations from artists due to a lack of opportunity. And as we shall see, these issues took in much more than music — looking at how we work together to impact all of our lives, for better and worse. But in all these stories and experiences, one thing that has also been apparent is that no matter where I've looked, worked or what I have done, I see how music makes places and lives better. I promise, if you take a second to look at music differently, as this book suggests, you will too.

CHAPTER 1
FOR SOMETHING TO EXIST, IT MUST HAVE A POLICY

In our towns, cities and places, are there regulations, policies and practices that threaten music, similar to how policy decisions we make end up poisoning water sources or lead to cracked pavements, unpaved roads and derelict houses? What intentionally makes music thrive, what harms it and what can be done to safeguard it? Lots can be done, but it requires intentionality to recognise music as an ecosystem and plan for it. Music is also a job for many — a complex, inequitable industry — and something that simultaneously binds us and tears us apart. In many cases, a city where music thrives is a city that thrives. So what if music was looked at intentionally in city planning? What impact would this have on our cities? To answer this, we must first outline what music is in this context.

Music is about more than a particular song in a particular moment. The success of music in a place demonstrates the success of a place in general. It shows an education system that taught music, that some sort of social safety infrastructure had to exist to convert taxpayer revenue into services such as nurseries, paved roads, working street lights, libraries and community centres. You need music venues that are economically viable. People have to be able to freely express themselves, no matter what they look like or what they believe. Residents need the time and disposable income to experience music. This leads to bands, DJs, composers and rappers recording, touring

5

and bringing revenue back to the community via retained earnings and tax receipts. If music thrives, so does the city.

Music is an effective canary in the development coal mine because it penetrates everything, and it can be, if we look at it differently, a way of creating better urban development policies. Planning, zoning, development and regeneration policies, the relationship between alcohol and law enforcement, a city's drive to recruit, retain and attract talent, the effectiveness of its tourism board — all are touched by music. So is affordable housing and issues of racial equity and justice.

Music is a tool we can use to measure how we communicate, how we govern, who we protect, who we discriminate against and how we co-exist together in our towns, cities and places. Music can promote or reduce fairness, from managing the impact of gentrification to measuring the impact of sustainable development around the world. Music is cultural, social and psychological currency, and the ecosystem that revolves around it mirrors and impacts the collective ecosystem that we share. Music can improve where we live, how we live and how we interact. We need to better understand how.

This lack of understanding comes from the fact that music is intensely personal. Music is *my music*, what *I listen to*, what *I like*. Even if I'm massively interested in music, not listening to it or engaging with it is a personal choice. I *choose* not to care too much about music. This personal relationship has birthed innumerate genres, disciplines and subcultures through the wide-ranging arrangement of sounds and tones. Music is a tool to better understand different cultures, dialects or viewpoints. Certain tones or pitches are recognisable to particular people. We associate bagpipes with Scotland or the flamenco guitar with Spain, despite bagpipes also being prevalent in Spain and flamenco music in Scotland. Our association of music aligns with our interpretation of a particular place or people. This can lead to implicit and explicit bias — such as associating metal music with satanism or rap with crime — colouring our perceptions of a place. I'll come to why this matters later, as music genres have been prioritised or criminalised due to these biases.

Rather than focusing on the singular pursuit — listening to the song — we should instead focus on the systems that enabled that song to make it to our ears. Whether it's the manufacturing of the instruments or the writing, recording and producing of the song, the creation of a data centre to house online files or the ability for artists to book live concerts, travel and perform in the flesh, it is all intertwined, and all of it requires rules and regulations to function in such a way that when you press play, you hear music.

Policy, by design, is impersonal — it is a blunt instrument that's meant to cover as much ground as possible. In order for legislators to legislate about something, it needs to exist. It must have a policy that outlines what it is, what it means, who it impacts and how it could and should be governed. For clean water, it's simple: we need it. Music is more complicated; it does not have a singular, all-encompassing policy outlining how it should be governed. Instead, it is pushed and pulled by a patchwork of policies — intellectual property law, zoning, noise ordinances, safety, policing, housing, redevelopment, economic growth, liquor, tourism and many more. There's nothing agreed across any level of government that outlines how music can be optimised as an ecosystem. Instead, we tend to govern music passively through other better-defined policy areas. A noise policy can include music, but it is about reducing or mediating noise; we incorporate some music into tourism and marketing initiatives, but measure success by heads in hotel beds and taxable receipts, not the impact of, or on, the music ecosystem. Music venues — even in the age of COVID-19 — remain important businesses to ensure cities remain open, vibrant and inclusive, but there's little guidance in building codes or other planning and zoning policies that outlines what a music venue could become or what its other community needs should be, or even what a music venue is defined as. It is a single, private business. One person's personal pursuit. Not a community benefit.

This is the *passive* policy problem with music, and it creates a policy environment where we do not use the music ecosystem to its fullest potential. Noise ordinances do the job well enough, education policy includes music as a voluntary subject and we're satisfied with that. But the impact of noise ordinances or education policy within the music ecosystem is ignored. We're happy to settle for mediocrity.

To understand how music impacts public policy, it needs to be broken into policy areas. How music impacts building codes, zoning, education, climate action or citywide strategic planning, recruiting and retaining talent and workers, the granting of planning permission or tourism and marketing plans. In all these sectors, music is usually absent from the discussion. Instead, it is seen as a creative pursuit, something that happens after work. It is not embedded in how we plan so that all things work better.

Let's take education policies as one example. You can learn music if you want to — it's not mandatory in most countries. But if you do choose to learn music, the genres open to you — as a result of the instruments on offer or the funding dedicated to the music curriculum — are more than often predetermined. Conversely, although education policy impacts music, the impact of music on overall education is rarely questioned. Will ensuring music education reaches everyone improve wider cognition, maths skills or interpersonal communication? Will teaching a wider variety of genres open up young minds to multiculturalism? These questions are rarely tabled, and this leads to a further lack of understanding of the role of music.

When there is no policy outlined about something, it does not exist in policy. In 2015, to explain the plight of small- to medium-sized music venues in the UK, after up to 30% of them had closed between 2005 and 2015, the Music Venue Trust charity created a definition of the term "Grassroots Music Venue".[1] Without it, a venue could be a stadium, arena, club, theatre or pub. Each policymaker imagined the word "venue" personally. The venue *I went to* is what a venue is. But venues could be churches, mosques, back rooms of pubs or arenas and everything in between. But it was a particular subset of venues in the UK that was in crisis — small- to medium-sized spaces that programmed three or four concerts per week. Without a policy to define what they were and why they needed assistance, the UK government was blind to their challenges. Once the definition was established and the term meant something, change was initiated to the point where planning law was amended to protect these venues. The creation of a policy, a definition, was integral. Without it, there wasn't a framework to fix the problem.

A First Look at Music's Role on Cities

A city is defined as having a high quality of life when living there is simple. Services function, rubbish is picked up, engaging with local government is seamless, schools are of high quality, crime is low and pollution is under control. This is reflected in the dozens of "quality of life" assessments and rankings published by magazines and consultancies each year. Take *Monocle* magazine, for example. Its Quality of Life survey for 2021 and 2022 names Copenhagen as the world's most liveable city.[2] In 2019 (there was no competition in 2020 due to the COVID-19 pandemic), it was Zurich,[3] which in 2021 and 2022 finished second. *Monocle*'s list prioritises European, northern hemisphere cities — no African, Latin American or American cities feature in the top twenty-five. Zurich is well managed and well governed and has vibrant arts and culture. With little fuss, a system of utilities, land management and local services functions for residents. Their taxes equate to services, including weekly rubbish removal or access to well-maintained green space. While the ranking does not mention Zurich's water filtration system as a benefit, it is world-leading.[4] It functions without incident and is so seamless that it isn't deemed worthy of note, but if it malfunctioned and Zurich's tap water became contaminated, it would immediately be talked about. Zurich's urban fabric would break down. The same goes for monitoring and managing air pollution or ensuring weekly rubbish removal. For people who live in cities where rubbish is not collected, it becomes a problem. A lack of functioning systems reduces one's quality of life, according to *Monocle*. This is why Zurich is often on top.[5]

Zurich is not known for its music scene. It did not invent house music, like Chicago, or incubate a renaissance in jazz, like New Orleans or Memphis. It has thriving music, nightlife and arts communities, but it is not known for them. But, like its sewage treatment plant and water filtration processes, Zurich's music scene — at least prior to the COVID-19 pandemic — functions. The city has an independent Night-Time Council, providing a governance mechanism for connecting its music venues and nightclubs with city government. It has robust licensing and planning policies, which govern opening hours, capacities, health and safety, and other needs. It hosts a global conference on governing the night economy. Its music and culture are open to all, residents and visitors alike. It enjoys a network of music and cultural festivals. It works because systems exist to support it — be it taxation, funding schemes, building maintenance or governance protocols. There is a music and nightlife policy framework, much like there's a water policy framework. And most of the time, we enjoy what it provides without noticing what went into maintaining it.

When the systems that bring us music work, we ignore them and enjoy the results. Places boast about their festivals, sons and daughters who went on to become famous artists, music heritage hotspots, the location of a famous album's recording or a legendary gig. But behind all this, an ecosystem must function to support it. And when it doesn't, it becomes a problem. As we have seen with the closure of music venues and cancellation of festivals due to the COVID-19 pandemic, and the challenges facing many premises and businesses, when the system breaks down for whatever reason, our access to music, in this case live music, is impacted. During a pandemic, the closure of venues and festivals is necessary; how we respond to this to provide assistance is voluntary. In many countries, including France, the Netherlands and Switzerland, the response was to provide relief to these businesses. In other countries, including the United States and Mexico, little, by comparison, was done, and many of these businesses have gone bankrupt at no fault of their own.

While every place — city, state or otherwise — uses music in some way, a policy to understand and support it is absent in intergovernmental, country, city, state and regional strategic plans. There is no music ecosystem policy framework in existence anywhere in the world, at any level of government. There is no music policy at the UN, IMF or World Bank. There are few conversations about music at the World Economic Forum. No country has a Minister for Music. Few cities have music officers. What benefits could a music ecosystem policy bring? We have a globally recognisable resource, a universal language that everyone understands that influences who we think we are, how we think and how we act, and we do not invest in understanding its overall impact on all of us. What would be better if we did?

One of My Favourite Bands

One of my favourite bands is Phish. They're relatively unknown outside the United States and Canada, but in North America they are superstars. Their headline concert in Florida at the turn of the millennium was the world's largest concert to welcome in that year. In 2017, the band performed 13 straight nights at New York's Madison Square Garden without repeating a song. They host festivals that welcome over 100,000 people — and they're the only act.

But what fascinates me most about Phish, and why I love the band, is how their music, aesthetic and outlook is intrinsically linked to the place they were founded — Burlington, Vermont. They talked about this in a podcast series about the band called *Long May They Run*, dedicating an episode to their relationship to their hometown.[6] When the band started out in 1983, Bernie Sanders was mayor. Despite a population of only 40,000, the city had a thriving arts, culture and music scene. The frigid temperatures during winter kept people inside, meaning more practice opportunities. For such a small place, it had more music venues per capita than anywhere else in the United States. Guitarist Trey Anastasio and bassist Mike Gordon have both said it wasn't possible for Phish to come from anywhere else. As a result, their music is peppered with references to their home city. Their major label debut in 1992 is named after the owner of the venue where they cut their teeth, Nectars. Songs reference local companies, such as "Harry Hood", which pays tribute to the local dairy. And to this day, Burlington is still a thriving music city. Nectars remains a local music venue and still hosts local bands.

In 2021, Jim Lockridge, the director of Burlington music non-profit Big Heavy World, and I launched a survey to better understand the city's local music economy. Despite Phish's legacy and other successful exports like Ben & Jerry's ice cream, musicians throughout Vermont were struggling. The median income for musicians and artists was below the local average of other sectors, Lockridge believed, and there were few mechanisms or policies to address the problem. So he wanted to compile a document containing the economic, social and cultural value of music to the city — along with recommendations for improving things. He would reveal the inequities and explain why it would be in the best interests of the city to address them.

I knew Phish had proselytised about Burlington, but had the city outlined its relationship with Phish, or with music in general? Along with tens of thousands of others, I have made the pilgrimage to the city, walked around the quaint city centre, and visited Nectars, imagining what it would have been like to see the band in such a small room. Probably *unlike* everyone else, I also wondered whether Burlington had any policies that would have made a band like Phish more likely to happen there than anywhere else. Did its public art programme, education policy, licensing framework or strategic plan have anything to do with it? Or did Phish *just happen*? Is it possible for a city to create a globally famous band? Can deliberate education, economic, social, cultural and tourism policies be designed to tilt the scales?

Phish thinks so, and they may have a point. In his eight years as mayor, Bernie Sanders pursued an agenda that fiercely promoted civic engagement, community activism and local organisation, much like other left-of-centre administrations. He spent money on arts and culture. He created a community development organisation. His staffer, Peter Clavelle, succeeded Sanders as mayor and — bar a two-year gap from 1993-95 — held the position until 2006. Investing in and the incubation of local businesses increased, and a land trust was created. A framework of governing focused on community empowerment, activism and engagement was created. Phish, along with Ben & Jerry's, Burton Snowboards and others came out of this political ideology. Burlington still has the nation's largest community-run supermarket. The local electric company is 100% renewable.

So if Burlington did it with Phish, why was Jim asking me for help to find out why musicians were struggling? No matter its successes, Burlington wasn't a paragon of music strategy. It went through economic hardship and budget cuts and, like most cities and governments, hadn't explored the role of the creative industry in its economic development.

What Jim wanted to know was: if Phish were right, can any city replicate that success? Can local policies, funding, practices and community engagement directly create a future rap superstar or leading jazz trio? And if the answer is yes, what are those policies? Are they all reliant on taxing and spending, or are they more nuanced? Who is the target recipient in each city? Would focusing on one, or a number of genres, lead to inequitable policy-making?

This is what Jim and I discussed. He wanted to know if a deliberate and intentional set of decisions — by policymakers, the community and musicians themselves — can create a better chance of investing in and incubating another Phish. The music industry chooses winners and losers. Can cities too? I believe the answer to these questions is "yes", and I'll explain why in this book.

What Is a Music Ecosystem Policy?

A music ecosystem policy is an overarching framework that encompasses the role of music across all governance structures, defining policies to support the creation, dissemination and enjoyment of music across society. It is not about any particular genre, discipline or outcome. The intention is to create a structure for better understanding the role and impact (positive and negative) of music on all policies.

If you weren't at the concert and had never heard of the band, you wouldn't notice the economic, social and cultural impact of that moment. If people don't understand the impact of a youth club to support emerging hip-hop, poetry and spoken word entrepreneurs and artists, why would they invest in it? If we can't stand metal, why celebrate it as cultural heritage? It's *their culture*, not *mine. My music is different.*

We can see an example of the results of this problem borne out in music education. Western countries still teach Western classical music to children as their introduction to music. But hip-hop is the world's most popular and widely listened-to music genre.[7] Few primary schools teach MC and DJ skills; instead, they shove pianos, violins, violas and cellos into young hands. This is not because pianos, violins, violas and cellos are more important. It is just historically, they are the instruments of choice for how we teach music, rather than two turntables and a microphone.

Zoom out and this cultural bias is written into our landscape. Many countries splash out on orchestral concert halls that few residents can afford to attend, in countries that lack rehearsal spaces for emerging DJs. It is because the political structures governing music prioritise certain instruments over others and because music is governed from an individual mindset, based on *"my music"*. In decision-making, one's personal relationship to music takes precedence over the needs of the music ecosystem. Over time, this impacts who has access to what, and where and how it impacts our urban environment. Making decisions based on *my personal musical choice* then gets reinforced historically, politically and in policy and through class- and race-based paradigms.

This mindset has seeped into how music interacts with policy. The problem we currently have is that music is incorporated into governing *when it suits*. If there's an issue that requires legislative change — such as protecting music venues in a dense town or city centre — we advocate for an alteration in planning law. This issue gets a lot of airtime, as most cities in the United States, Canada, Europe, the UK and Australia are seeing music venues and nightclubs close down for a variety of reasons.

Implementing a policy governing the wider ecosystem is much more efficient and effective than a reactive approach to challenges when they appear. Venues being threatened by new housing developments or artists or copyright holders not receiving their fair share from the usage of their music are symptoms of a lack of music ecosystem policies, even though they are treated as one-offs.

Here's another example: music as a tool for cognitive development is well researched. From listening to classical music when pregnant to engaging babies and children in songs for learning the alphabet, music is an accepted and powerful educational tool. As children get older, learning an instrument increases their ability to analyse complex thoughts, play well with others and be empathetic. Playing music as part of a group encourages discipline, while singing in a choir supports vocal cord development, literacy and linguistic skills. But there are no globally recognised, researched and tested policies enacted by all levels of government that demonstrate the value of music in education and legislate for its development.

Music also affects where we live, particularly for those lucky enough who can choose. For those who go to university, often the music and cultural scenes of a place are as much of a draw as the quality of education. Between 2020 and 2050, the world's urban population is expected to grow by 2.5 billion, an addition of about 170,000 people a day.[8] Although job opportunities are the most significant driver of people to urban areas, the cultural and music offer included is also important. Music is part of what drives mass urbanisation.

And although we know people move to cities to experience culture and nightlife, policy-makers don't pay sufficient attention to the infrastructure required for a thriving cultural scene. When it works, we call a place "vibrant". When it doesn't, it is chaotic or dangerous. When the music is not to someone's taste, it can increase fear and biased decision-making. When a person can't sleep, they are irritable. So when things go wrong, it's personal situation versus personal situation — those who want to go out against those who want to sleep. The urban environment becomes polarised, and music, in one way or another, is part of the problem.

Rather than tackling these issues on a case-by-case basis, we should explore why there's no foresight being applied — why isn't there a music ecosystem policy? People should be able to sleep in their apartment, even if there's a concert going on downstairs. Gig-goers should be able to park without being grossly overcharged or ticketed, or have a safe night-time public transport option available. Those who want quiet should have it.

What benefits would a music ecosystem policy bring? Would it encourage or make apparent that it is of equal importance to have policies that encourage, educate, train and support those who work to create music, on and off stage? Of course it would. Let's look at how that might work in practice.

Introducing the Music City

To begin to think about how a city would function if it had a policy to better understand and grow its music ecosystem, let's look at how music is considered within city policy circles now.

The overarching term used to refer to a city that is deemed to have an active and engaged relationship with music is "Music City". A quick Google search reveals a host of travel and tour operators offering trips to experience America's Music Cities, usually defined as Nashville, Memphis and New Orleans. Each of these places has a relationship with the history of the nation's popular music. They all incubated famous artists and are known for their buzzing live music scenes. They're Music Cities because each has a defined relationship with the artform predicated on what has happened in the past and how it is used as a marketing tool to attract tourists. Each is unique. There are no comparable experiences of bar-hopping on Beale Street on a Saturday night or Mardi Gras in New Orleans or a honky-tonk in Nashville. Music is part of their urban fabric.

The earliest example of a city deliberately and intentionally aligning itself with music in one way or another is Nashville, Tennessee. Since 2007, the city's convention and visitors bureau has owned the legal trademark of "Nashville Music City", for business management and business administration purposes.[9] But to understand the importance of this term, we have to go back to its origins.

The term "Music City" dates back to the early 1800s when Nashville had a modest but active group of businesses creating and reproducing sheet music. The Fisk Jubilee

Singers, a local *a cappella* group, were the first musical group to complete a world tour. This was a revelation for those who saw them perform, and it created a mythology around the city where it was assumed the group was one of many. A century after the Fisk Jubilee Singers' tour, it was an insurance company that helped cement Nashville's "Music City" branding and the creative output that came with it.

In 1925, the National Life Accident and Insurance Company owned a local radio station called WSM (We Shield Millions).[10] To encourage more people to purchase insurance, the station promoted the popular culture of the time — country music — on its airwaves every Saturday. These live performances happened in the local concert hall, the Grand Ole Opry, and while many cities had radio stations broadcasting live music shows at the time, the Opry became the most popular. With every broadcast, Nashville's reputation as a centre for music creation, production and talent was enhanced. Like all successful shows, it developed a fanbase. People wanted to travel to Nashville to get as close to the source as possible. And so the Grand Ole Opry became a tourist attraction, even though the main purpose of the concerts was to sell insurance.

Craig Havighurst, in *Air Castle of the South: WSM and the Making of Music City,* argues that the "Music City" moniker was accidental. Although the initial purpose of WSM was selling insurance, music became a tool for engaging residents and promoting community cohesion. The more listeners the station had, the more potential customers it reached. Havighurst writes:

> When WSM went on air, nobody outside of Nashville could have predicted, and few inside of Nashville would have wished, that the city would become a haven for show business... songs were written and performed in New York and Chicago. Movies came from Hollywood. If the nation

had a country music center, it was arguably Atlanta, a town nearly twice the size of Nashville.[11]

The city's success snowballed. As buying a radio became cheaper, more and more people tuned in. Then television became accessible, and the weekly show was broadcast locally, expanding its audience further. Throughout the late 1940s and 1950s, the growing popularity and reach of the Grand Ole Opry saw country music hopefuls pack up and move to Nashville. By the end of the 1950s, there was a critical mass of songwriters and performers in the city. While the success of the Grand Ole Opry and its home in Nashville could not have been predicted, another factor supported the development of Nashville as a Music City — its local plan.

Nashville had a low building density, no high rises and expansive land plots for residential developments, which provided musicians with the space to make noise without upsetting their neighbours. Housing lots were more spread out than in other major centres, and palatable weather made it attractive to live there, record and relax. In addition, the city was, as Ken Burns argued, a good place to begin a tour, as it's a ten-hour drive from most American metropolises outside the West Coast.[12]

However, the term "Nashville Music City" was not trademarked by its Convention and Visitors Bureau (tourism board) until 2008.[13] Until then, the Music City branding grew organically, rather than deliberately. As the music business expanded from the 1970s to the 1990s with the introduction of cassette tapes, compact discs and a more accessible touring framework, Nashville leveraged its Music City reputation, even without owning the brand. Global record labels and music publishing companies set up offices in Nashville alongside performing rights organisations. A square mile on 16th Ave in the Edgehill

District became known as Music Row, because its buildings were home to an inordinate number of music studios and record labels. The studios built in these modest residential units captured the voices and sounds of Chet Atkins, Dolly Parton, Elvis Presley and thousands of others, defining American popular music and, in the process, generating tens of billions of dollars. Nashville competed with global entertainment powerhouses such as New York, London and Los Angeles, despite being much smaller. A city of 700,000 people became the world's premier Music City.

RCA Studios, courtesy of Michael Ochs archives.[14]

At last count, in 2019, Nashville's music industry supported 16,298 jobs, but it's estimated that over 60,000 people work across the music ecosystem or are supported by it in one way or another.[15] The city has, in the past, convened an advisory Music City Music Council, run by a mayoral appointee, to manage the relationship between the city and the sector. While it has been dormant since 2019, work is underway to relaunch it in some form or fashion. Nashville is the undisputed home of the country music industry, hosting its awards, museum and a vast majority of its songwriters. It is estimated 82 people move to Nashville every day,[16] and it still boasts the third-largest music industry in the United States behind New York City and Los Angeles.

Nashville claims its title as *the* Music City, both due to its trademarking of the brand and use of it across marketing, but also the significant music sector that remains there and its importance as a place to write, record and perform. The local government also invests in policies and structures to better understand the impact of music on the city. Every decade, through its Chamber of Commerce, an economic impact report on the value of music takes place. Just recently, the city council approved $2m in federal relief funding to support music venues impacted by a devastating tornado that ripped through parts of the city in early 2020 and COVID-19.[17] A further $300,000 was allocated from federal relief money to study music venues in 2022.[18]

But Nashville has a number of challenges in its music strategy. For one, it has not approached its policy-making in a way that recognises music as an ecosystem. Instead, it sees it as a brand to be protected and exploited. A century after WSM took to the airwaves, one of the most storied recording studios — RCA Studio A — required private intervention to avoid demolition, while Music Row is one of the most at-risk areas of national heritage, according to the National Trust for Historic Preservation.[19] Nashville's zoning policies — in place since 1998 — prohibited residential properties being used for commercial business, which affected a number of home recording studios (as well as tutors, hair stylists and others). [20] This was amended in 2020, but in effect made it difficult to set up a home studio in Nashville for over two decades.

In 2017, Nashville Metro Public Schools cited "music education neglect" in its teaching framework, despite partnerships with the Country Music Association, Grammy Music Education Coalition and others.[21] There are campaigns advocating for greater inclusion of other genres in the city's music promotion strategy, as Nashville is home to as much hip-hop as it is country, even if honkytonks and dive bars dominate Broadway.[22] Its hip-hop scene is referred to as *underground*, a code word for underappreciated or undervalued. At the same time, systemic racism continues to challenge the country music ecosystem. In the aftermath of the murder of George Floyd in Minneapolis, Mickey Guyton, a Black, Nashville-based country artist, participated in a webinar about being African-American in Nashville's music industry, reported on by the *Washington Post*:

> She and other members of the Nashville community spoke candidly about what they go through that their white colleagues would never consider, including feeling alienated from the country genre, the fear when they see Confederate flags and tattoos, and using caution when travelling in rural areas. One music executive recounted being called "coloured" and the person defending the remark by explaining, "I'm from the country, and that's just what we call you."[23]

Like all cities, the built environment changes in Nashville — music venues close and new ones open. However, the city has not extensively mapped its music infrastructure, which leaves its planning framework susceptible to a reduction in music- and culture-related infrastructure. By not knowing what exists, where it is and what measures will be needed in five, ten or 15 years' time, there's little protection, preservation or planning of Nashville's music ecosystem.

This is happening on Music Row, where 50 buildings that were home to music-related uses have been demolished since 2013.[24]

Few of these challenges are unique to Nashville, but it remains the only place that trademarks itself on being the "Music City". This means more than the success of a music business or being able to use the end product to market goods, services or business attraction. But it can only do so if music's impact is better understood as an ecosystem, rather than as a marketing platform or singular genre-specific industry. Nashville's moniker may have grown organically, but other cities are taking a more deliberate approach to using music as a tool for growth. One of the most successful is Austin, Texas.

A Deliberate Invention: Live Music Capital of the World

Austin used music as a method of attracting talent and investment to create economic growth. As a result, it is now known as the "Live Music Capital of the World". The origins of the branding are disputed, but began as early as 1985 as outlined by the Austin Chamber of Commerce ad in *Billboard* magazine, discovered by a local journalist, Mose Buchele.[25]

The city's lively live music scene was supported by a large university (the University of Texas at Austin) and the close proximity of music bars and clubs in its central business district. In 1987, 177 artists converged on Austin for the inaugural South by Southwest (SXSW) music festival, which has grown to be the largest music festival and conference in the world.[26] In the following three decades, Austin became the United States' fastest growing city of over a million people.[27] Music is not the only reason this has happened. Austin's climate, location near many large population centres and status as a capital city have played a role, but the prolonged and structured use of music as a way of attracting business, visitors and artists is a success. This creates winners and losers. Austin is now one of the most profitable cities in the United States for short-term rental providers, but its local musicians and creative communities are facing an affordability crisis.[28] These challenges have been recognised by Austin City Council and a host of local community groups, resulting in the creation of one of the most robust music ecosystem policy infrastructures of any city in the world.

Austin has not been universally successful, but it acted deliberately to use music within urban governance and city growth. It has a staffed city music office and set up many organisations to support musicians and creators. In 2016, a Creative Space and Assistance Program (CSAP) was launched to help artists and creators by subsidising work and recording spaces, with a budget of $750,000.[29] Austin has a local healthcare non-profit specific to musicians, a number of foundations exist to invest in music and the city has a team of full-time staff dedicated to music and the night-time economy across city government. Urban planning, regeneration, alcohol and liquor licensing, workforce development, tourism, health and social care and incentive policies all include or refer to music in some way.

The city conducted a wide-ranging music census in 2014 to determine the economic, social and cultural challenges of its musicians and music professionals. Another has since been completed in 2022, through a third-party, rather than the city itself.[30] It allocated a portion of its Hotel Occupancy Taxes (HOT) to support a broad range of uses related to commercial music marketing and music tourism. In 2019, the tax was increased by .2 cents per room, per night, to help fund the expansion of Austin's convention center. Of the .2 cent increase, 15% was allocated to music specifically, an amount estimated as $3m per year.[31] This policy is one of the most progressive in the world, as there is often little appetite for funding talent development and music marketing, minus creating signage or brand campaigns for music.

Moreover, the city acted swiftly to support its music venues and musicians impacted by COVID-19. While far from sufficient, the city allocated $6m in federal relief money for its music ecosystem.[32] This has not saved every venue from closure, but it is far more support than most other cities allocated during the pandemic. Specific grant programmes have been introduced by private organisations, each set up to support and promote different parts of Austin's music ecosystem.

However, its success as the "Live Music Capital of the World" hasn't been great for many of those responsible for creating the content that supports this brand. Of those who responded to the census in 2014, 70% earned less than $10,000 per year and only 22% engaged in music as their full-time career.[33] Like all cities, as *NPR* reported in 2015, "the division within Austin's local music industry can be taken as a microcosm of the effects that technological globalisation has on artists and creators."[34] Sectors one step removed from the creation of music — tech, gaming, video — grew in Austin. Google, Facebook and Apple now have offices there, and the city added 5,200 tech jobs in 2018.[35] Apple was offered $36m in incentives in 2012 for its first campus in the city.[36] These deals are common, with property tax abatements (i.e., a company not paying property tax) often used as an incentive to attract investment. Apple's promise to invest $1bn was offered on the following conditions:

In exchange for investing $400m in purchasing the land and developing the campus as well as creating 4,000 new jobs, Williamson County (in Austin's outskirts) would abate or reimburse 65% of ad valorem taxes for real and business personal property for 15 years, according to the proposed terms of the agreement.[37]

Austin, unlike other cities, took steps to understand, measure and assuage the impact of this growth. While it struggled to ensure that musicians benefited from urban growth, institutional investment and regeneration, it produced data to understand the impact on its music ecosystem. It employs staff as liaisons, researchers and policy advisors.

Throughout this growth, the tagline remained, but Austin's affordability for its musicians and creatives shrank. In 2018, its income inequality was rising faster than that of the state of Texas.[38] Austin is still rated better than others, with an inequality ranking below most of America's five hundred largest cities,[39] but the rising cost of living is not equalled by higher performance fees or IP return. Musicians' income stagnated despite the cost of living increasing. This was more pronounced in communities of colour, including the Black and Latinx communities, where the divide grew sharper than it did for white Austinites.[40]

Still, Austin carries on being the Live Music Capital of the World. A stroll down 6th Street, its hub of live music venues, bars and speakeasies, reflects that. In a city of 1.5 million people, prior to the COVID-19 shutdown, Austin hosted over 100 shows a night. It is back to hosting this number of concerts each weekend again.

Still, the authorities were slow to act to support music venues and musicians during the pandemic, leading to musicians calling for the Live Music Capital of the World branding to be rescinded.[41] Although $5m was allocated to struggling businesses, the needs of the city's 54 music venues is almost $4m per month for rent and salaries alone.[42] Venues have closed, businesses have laid off staff and the city has not responded in the manner the music ecosystem expected. Three decades of music ecosystem policy didn't stem the crisis. By comparison, the state of Oregon allocated $50m to its music venues, theatres and performance spaces.[43] Austin and Oregon's music economies are similar. Oregon's is worth $1.72bn, supporting 27,000 jobs in the recorded music industry, according to the Recording Industry Association of America (RIAA), in 2018.[44] Austin's is worth $1.6bn, at last count in 2016.[45]

Paying attention to its music ecosystem and using it as a tool to attract talent, investment and tourists does not make a city more equitable or, in many cases, a better place to pursue a career in music. In some cases, the opposite was becoming true, if the findings in the Austin music census were to be internalised. The more successful a Music City becomes, the harder it is to sustain its core musical community and the spontaneous magic that led to the brand meaning something in the first place. This makes investing in music as an ecosystem more prevalent. This is true for all artforms, but recognisable across all music, even though some genres impact cities more than others. For example, the Austrian city of Salzburg — Mozart's birthplace — is 4% more expensive than Graz, a hotbed of experimental jazz and electronic music, which doesn't have the same acclaim as its neighbour.[46]

Both Nashville and Austin are living labs for music ecosystem policy, but their actions and initiatives are not wholly replicable, nor should they be seen as what a model policy could be. In some way, the success of Austin and Nashville deterred other cities from looking seriously at music ecosystem policy. Austin and Nashville, maybe New Orleans, New York, Memphis, Detroit, Seattle and Los Angeles, are considered *the Music Cities* in the United States;

these are the ones with concentrations of music industries. These are the cities that are marketed by tour operators to go to and experience *a taste of America's Music Cities*. It's not that Tulsa or Fort Worth or Louisville don't have thriving music scenes and musicians with the same aspirations as those in Nashville or Austin or concentrations of industry; they do — it's just they aren't seen as *Music Cities*.

This is the difference between being a Music City and pursuing music ecosystem policies within other civic governance and structures. You don't need one to have the other. Income inequality, racial justice and a thriving music scene exist in Wilmington, Delaware or Winnipeg, as much as they do in Austin and Nashville. Yes, only one city can claim being the Live Music Capital of the World, but every city has a music ecosystem. All cities can better understand them, advocate for them and create positive, proactive policies to better understand their role across the built environment.

Imagine having forewarning of problems that might occur and a plan to deal with them. What would it be like to have a music resilience plan for the urban environment, where the value of music is maximised to reach as many citizens as possible? In a world where only a few cities — less than 1% at last count — use their music ecosystems as a way of getting to grips with the success or failures of civic governance, this is an opportunity.

Blindly emulating Nashville and Austin leaves cities vulnerable to celebrating the value of music without recognising the need to understand, build and support the infrastructure required to sustain it.

Music's role in cities is as multifaceted as any other form of human interaction. It is not simply a marketing tool or a platform for business attraction. It is also not the sole responsibility of non-profit organisations or multinational music companies. As an ecosystem, music is a form of social and physical infrastructure. It requires a place and a mindset in order to thrive. If forced into situations, it can cause harm; if properly planned, it can be transformational. But music is not seen this way. Many global cities are either music cities by heritage or association. Cities like New Orleans, Chicago, Detroit and St Louis, Kansas City and Memphis in the United States are the origins of key advancements in the development of American music. Seoul is known for k-pop and Kobe for northern soul. Liverpool has the Beatles and Amsterdam has techno. Mumbai has Bollywood music and Montreal, throughout the early 2000s, was home to the resurgence of Canadian indie rock. But few of these cities treat music as infrastructure, and most, as a result, lack the resources to support their music ecosystems. Like Austin and Nashville, all have seen their music venues and musicians suffer as a result of restrictions due to COVID-19, inflation and the increase in the cost of living.

Equally, it is a misnomer to discount any city, town or place as not having a music ecosystem worth investing in. This is not about the size of the city, but the principles in play. Where there are people, there's music, and no matter the scale, music ecosystem policies have a place, from small villages to large metropolises. The town of Bee Cave outside of Austin is as musical as its larger neighbour in many regards. Those who live there experience music, whether it's in their cars, homes and out at local restaurants. What usually happens when places don't have a policy for music is a hodgepodge of arts subsidies for festivals or orchestras. But the investments aren't tied together or linked within a wider ecosystem. Music is celebrated for just a few days a year.

Nonetheless, what's on the stereo, how it gets there and how it impacts our urban geographies is still impacted by the decisions made in city governments, even if the word "music" is not included in decision-making. By not understanding the sound and acoustics of our urban fabric, we pass noise bylaws that restrict music in places, despite not measuring the impact this would have on the music ecosystem. We expect our arenas and stadiums to be filled with fans of global superstars, and celebrate when they emerge from our hometowns, but we fail to grasp the impact that reducing music education has on this happening. We expect people to live in denser communities, and those who do so expect to have a vibrant quality of life — until it gets too loud and they can't sleep. Music is delivered on demand, when and where we want it, yet in many countries, policies to pay those who create the music do not exist. We need music. We need infrastructure. We do not put them together.

According to cultural theorist Richard Florida and academic Michael Seman, the US is estimated to lose 2.7 million jobs and more than $150bn in the creative businesses due to the pandemic. These figures represent 50% of all jobs in those industries and more than a quarter of all sales nationwide.[47] The greatest falls are in cities with higher concentrations of music and creative workers, including New York, Austin and Nashville. At the same time, more cities and countries are exploring the role of music and the arts as a way of recovering faster. Many cities in the United States have and continue to allocate relief funding to music.[48] The French, Dutch, German and Nordic governments are supporting their music festivals, venues and professionals. While there is profound displacement and job losses, an opportunity to further assert and define the role of music ecosystems in urban environments has emerged. In some places, this is a build from scratch. Others are tearing down and rebuilding. We need an overarching set of policies to assert the value that music ecosystems can bring, and the policy tools needed for all cities to emerge stronger, rather than devoid of venues, artists and musicians. If we had that, maybe we would collectively create more jobs than lose half of them as predicted.

Music Ecosystems for All

Austin and Nashville are initial examples because they dominate the discourse about what a Music City or music ecosystem is. Both cities have taken deliberate and intentional views that music, in all its forms and functions, is part of the city's DNA. But in doing so, winners are chosen, which creates losers over time. This is because, in both cities, certain aspects of music, such as live music or branding a city through music to encourage economic development, are prioritised. Other elements of the music ecosystem, such as education or zoning and regulation, may not be prioritised as much, which creates a pendulum effect when music becomes successful in one aspect of city-building; in doing so, it can often reveal inequalities in other parts of the ecosystem. Nashville, for example, has focused on its relationship with country music to the point that a trade association emerged to differentiate workers in other genres, called The Other Nashville Society.[49] And just because a city focuses on or promotes itself with music, it does not mean that music is optimised across the community, in each neighbourhood, school and park. Nashville and Austin are leaders in creating the model for a front-facing, promotional Music City, and have reaped the economic rewards that brings, but their commendable efforts also reveal a myth; that a city needs to be promoted as a *Music City* to be a city that treats music robustly and effectively in how it creates sustainable, positive governance for its citizens. Promoting music, being a front-facing *Music City*, is not a collective, overarching framework. It is part of the story, but not the whole story. Windhoek or

Nur-Sultan can learn from Austin or Nashville; but without an overarching framework, these lessons could be difficult to implement. Like Nashville or Austin, there's plenty of music in both Namibia and Kazakhstan.

This becomes apparent when something bad happens. A venue closes, or in the case of Austin and every other city in the world, a pandemic forces all venues to close. The inequities inherent in the system, where decisions are made to support certain initiatives, communities and objectives over others, are laid bare. Having a robust live music scene is welcome, but if all those working in it rely on cash-in-hand, point-of-sale income to sustain themselves, the entire economy collapses if those venues close, despite music not disappearing from society. In fact, music usage increased while at the same time some of those responsible for it were driven into poverty and financial ruin, even in those cities deemed the most musical in the world. This is the difference between promoting oneself via music and creating a robust music ecosystem policy that encompasses music in all its forms and functions. If these artists had a larger share of revenue of their music that was being listened to online or on the radio, it might have supported the loss of live concert revenue. If more musicians were registered as limited companies or were recognised by chambers of commerce or economic development departments, finding and supporting them as businesses may have been simpler. But in most places, this wasn't the case. What should have been, may have been, has never been — in Austin or Nashville, or anywhere for that matter. The ecosystem was recognised in some respects, but not all.

Music does not exist in a vacuum, and its impact on cities and places has been analysed before, primarily in investigations into the impact of the creative economy on urban growth, regeneration and gentrification. What's different here is that a thriving Music City, town or place is one that recognises it as an ecosystem, rather than festivals, venues and heritage alone. It's not just about growing a music industry or having a flagship music festival. It's about music making places better, through the people that live and work there.

If musicians can't survive in cities, there's a good chance most other creators face the same problems. If we lack music education in our schools, we're creating children that are worse-off creatively. And for all this to work, we need a policy to understand it, support it and measure it. This has become more evident in the fallout from the COVID-19 pandemic and the increased pressures that inflation and the cost of living have engendered, but can be traced to a decade before, where decisions made in both Melbourne and Sydney in Australia created paradoxical case studies about how music impacts cities, and how to create and implement policies that make places better through music, rather than focusing on one specific aspect of music, which can often make things worse.

CHAPTER 2
MUSIC ECOSYSTEMS FOR ALL?

Every community engages with music differently. As discussed, if there is a notable, recognisable heritage, often seeing music more as part of a city's identity or branding is more prevalent. When music is not as popular, it may be less regarded as a tool for city development, despite its existing in much the same manner as an ecosystem. In all cities, to some extent, people are learning, playing and enjoying music. But the ways in which governments have become engaged in music ecosystem policy, especially since the early 2010s, can be best understood in two case studies, that of Melbourne and Sydney. And in both cases, music became entangled in issues unrelated to but impacting on the city's wider strategic growth. And in both cases, it had little to do with music.

Save Live Australia's Music

On 23 February 2010, in the middle of a hot, sticky Australian summer, over 20,000 people marched through the streets of Melbourne with placards and banners, protesting in support of live music. The rally, titled "Save Live Australia's Music", or SLAM, was the largest show of music-related protest and civil disobedience ever in Australia.

The ability to perform and experience live music, at that moment, was not under threat. The night before, Melbourne — the capital of the state of Victoria — hosted more than 100 gigs, from cover bands in dive bars to a few national and international acts. One of those who attended a gig that night was the editor of *The Age*, *Sydney Morning Herald*'s entertainment guide, named Paddy. Paddy was not a regular protester. But he and other music fans had had enough, and it all started, like most large-scale protests, with a single event.

One of Melbourne's most storied venues is the Tote Hotel, located in Collingwood, an inner-city suburb. The Tote was built in 1876, providing low-cost accommodation to the area's workers and travellers, and for three decades from 1980, it was home to Melbourne's emerging indie, punk and rock communities, becoming one of the city's main jumping-off points for local talent.

To many, however, the Tote was just a run-down bar and music venue. Collingwood was developing quickly and required more housing — particularly for the influx of the sort of people who wanted to live close to the city's central business district but in an area that retained a slight grittiness. Collingwood in 2010, like many other areas, was home to immigrants, lower-income residents and artists. It was a centre of Melbourne's industrial past. It retained its mid-nineteenth-century industrial architecture; factories and large warehouses dotted the neighbourhood, providing ideal spaces for artists, musicians and noisy activities such as recording studios, rehearsal spaces and music with the venues.[1] Collingwood had a thriving music ecosystem, even if its existence occurred without any planning. The infrastructure, location and architecture made it a desirable place to live and work if one was pursuing music or other artforms. Without any formal policy or understanding, it had become a Music City within Melbourne.

Some of the music incubated at the Tote became globally renowned, but in 2010, citing high costs due to restrictive licensing conditions, licensee Bruce Milne decided to close the venue. He told *The Age*:

> The high-risk conditions they have placed on the Tote's licence make it impossible to trade profitably. I can't afford the new high-risk fees they have imposed. I can't afford to keep fighting them at VCAT. I can't renegotiate a lease in this environment.[2]

VCAT is the statutory body that governs disputes related to decisions made by Liquor Licensing Victoria, the regional licensing body that determined the price that venue leaseholders paid to be able to sell alcohol. Although it had existed since the late 1990s, by 2009 Liquor Licensing Victoria was enforcing "special conditions", specifically tied to venues that sell alcohol and have live or amplified music, and VCAT was upholding them. Although these conditions, which required CCTV cameras and a minimum of two bouncers where "live or amplified recorded music" is played, had been in place for almost two decades, it was only from 2009 that they had been enforced. This was because — as the *Sydney Morning Herald* reported — of a statistical increase in what was referred to as "alcohol-fuelled violence".[3]

In 2009 and 2010, some high-profile alcohol-influenced incidents occurred in Melbourne. According to the Australian Institute of Health and Welfare, the number of victims of alcohol-related physical abuse increased from 4.5% in 2007 to 8.1% in 2010, of total incidents recorded.[4] "It's not that there isn't a problem with alcohol like there is in a lot of other places," remarked Paddy, reflecting on the public's mood at the time. "But instead of looking at the problem in a structured way, it was decided to impose more restrictions on bars and pubs. And for some reason we will never know, it was decided that bars and pubs with music were the worst offenders."[5]

What was happening in Collingwood was a pattern of gentrification that is repeated in many cities across the globe. In her book *The Great Music City*, Andrea Baker chronicled the challenges surrounding the Tote by contextualising it geographically as part of a set of particular conditions that were expanding throughout the region north of the Yarra River, outside of downtown Melbourne. Baker notes that, as early as the late 1990s, a single complaint from a new apartment block led to the closure of another venue, the Empress Hotel.[6] According to one of the local business owners and operators Baker interviewed, Helen Marcou AM of Bakehouse Studios, music began to be vilified in the media. Speaking to Baker, Marcou noted it was an election year, and law and order proved to be an effective election strategy. Live music, Marcou said, was an easy target to appeal to a more conservative voter base.[7]

Marcou AM and her partner, Quincy McLean AM, opened Bakehouse Studios in 1991 and were instrumental in the creation of Save Live Australia's Music and changes that emerged from it. The location of the studio, in the heart of Yarra, placed them in the middle of the challenges that emerged with the Tote, as similar development was happening around their studio. It was on their insistence that a protest be held and that it be called Save Live Australia's Music, rather than Save Live Australian Music, so as to be as inclusive as possible whilst recognising the country's racist, colonial past.

At the same time, Collingwood was changing, as all areas do when they begin to experience external investment and gentrification. The neighbourhood was being viewed differently, depending on what one's objectives were. If one were a residential property developer, edginess was welcome to a point. To others, any new development was a threat, regardless of the need for housing. Music was in the middle of Collingwood's evolution, but it was not taken at face value, understood and incorporated into the changes, according to studio owners like Marcou AM. At the same time, as with all changing neighbourhoods, those enforcing the change needed someone or something to blame. The situation worsened from there.

The Tote announced its closure, and the thousands of people who spontaneously gathered to protest forced the street to be closed by police. The need for increased regulation of live music and access to alcohol was not acceptable to the protestors and local music businesses such as Bakehouse; they felt the correlation between music and so-called alcohol-fuelled violence, and the government's use of it to target bars and pubs, was a simple re-election tactic and a tool to support private development's interests. Two months later, over 20,000 people joined a more organised march to protest not only its closure, but the perceived threat to live music throughout Victoria.

Venues like the Tote exist in every major city, and though through popular protest the Tote has been "saved", many others have become blocks of flats, restaurants or clothing stores. Some venues are readily described as legendary, but even the most famous ones aren't safe. In New York City, there was CBGBs; in Manchester, the Hacienda; in London, the Luminaire; Toronto, the Comfort Zone. These venues, or memories of them at least, are everywhere.

Melbourne: Live Music Capital of the World?

Melbourne is synonymous with music, art and culture. When calculated in 2018, the city had more live music venues than any other in the world with a population of more than one million people.[8] It has a renowned classical music tradition, and a recognised and celebrated popular heritage. Nick Cave is from Melbourne. AC/DC spent their formative years living there and wrote and recorded their first two albums in the city. More recently, local Courtney Barnett put the Melbourne drawl and inflated property prices on the global stage with her charming indie rock.

Not all of its music citizens were born in Melbourne, but most moved there because of its supportive ecosystem bound by a truckload of venues, indie labels and popular and supportive community radio. Despite that, however, Victoria was the only state in the country without a music representative peak body, and as it didn't yet have a strong united voice, more than 20,000 people had to march on the streets to be heard and — according to them — save live music.

Music was a key contributor to city quality of life in 2010, and Collingwood's growth was linked to the development of its local art, music and cultural scenes. The area became desirable because people living there created interesting things and the Tote operated within a familiar ecosystem for three decades. The encroachment of other needs — housing, a desire to live close to the centre, investing in real estate and ensuring that it brought a return to the landowner — grew alongside it, but there was no communication or understanding of how the existing ecosystem in Collingwood functioned and how these changes related to the cultural activities already there. This is not a Melbourne-specific problem. The same issues exacerbate ethnic or cultural displacement and occur in neighbourhoods all over the world, with the value of land trumping the value of what was happening in its buildings. This is the paradox of much gentrification — music was an economic generator, a cultural draw that gave an area its bohemian and exciting character to new arrivals, but it was also a nuisance.

There were a number of implicit biases in place that led to music fans marching that day. The first was a correlation between live music and alcohol-fuelled violence. The term "alcohol-fuelled violence" itself is inherently problematic, because it transfers the blame for the incident from the individual to the substance. Attaching music as an accelerant is equally questionable. We're being asked to assume that live music is an activity that propels or speeds up drunkenness, and those who watch live music are more prone to fighting. The second bias implied that live music is a fringe activity in our cities, not one that's welcomed into the collective fabric of urban infrastructure. It suggested that live music can only exist in places that do not prioritise housing; it is a luxury, not a necessity. The impression is that if more houses are needed, live music must get out of the way. It's something to be enjoyed by others — people who are mainly there to get drunk. When you see the live music attendee as other, then their needs are seen to contradict people who agree with us. This bias is systemic in how live music venues or other for-profit businesses that trade in culture are considered. One of the most impacted sectors around the world due to the COVID-19 pandemic was live music venues, nightclubs and bars. In many places, they received no state support to subsist, despite being unable to trade. Live music or clubbing is fun. It is nice to have. It's not a real business.

In some ways, this is the most pernicious bias. It believes that these types of businesses — in this case, bars and pubs that host live music or DJs — are not as reputable as those in other sectors. It instils a double standard, made worse because policies meant to create fairness or a framework to debate regulations don't exist for music. Music is governed through other policy lenses, such as laws relating to alcohol consumption, noise and environmental health. This prejudice is particularly visible when it comes to noise complaints. In the UK, neighbours complain about noise every 80 seconds.[9] More than 80% of registered noise complaints are residential. To reduce this, we could ban homes — it would certainly solve the problem. That might sound facetious, but this is the heavy-handed thinking attached to live music. A lack of policy to better understand the music ecosystem makes this worse.

Living in cities, we accept a reasonable amount of noise as a fact of daily life. Living near a train line is a reality many accept in London, even though freight trains are frequent at 3am. It's a familiar story across America's Midwest — despite the noise, trains continue to operate at night and have created eminent domain policies that permit them to do so. In Victoria in 2010, if one neighbour complained about a music venue, even if the venue was in business before the neighbour moved in, the complaint could result in the venue being closed or facing stricter, more expensive licensing conditions. Music venues are simply not seen as important.

The problem with the Tote arose because music was being governed by policies unrelated to Melbourne's music ecosystem at the time. Essentially, the city hadn't planned for music; it had happened by accident, and because live music was so intrinsically linked to alcohol sales (which essentially pay for the bands and infrastructure), the government considered it a vice, offering as much cultural merit as a strip club or casino. In this sense, music was being damaged by the unintended consequences of a crackdown on other vices. Unlike other businesses or traditional industries such as manufacturing, banking and healthcare, most city policies consider live music and the places that incubate it as leisure uses, not legitimate business uses. As a result, the jobs, skills and trades that are housed in these places, from manning a soundboard or managing a bar to dealing with security or performing on stage, are not counted as jobs to be created, safeguarded and promoted. Many of these jobs are cash-in-hand, hence the term "gig economy", and as a result are not represented in GDP figures.

Finally, another bias that persists is that music venues tend to prioritise the young and ignore the old. The young do not vote as much as the old, and when they do, they tend to vote for more liberal policies. In 2010, the Victorian, left-of-centre Labor Party was running for re-election. It would make sense for them to court younger and more diverse voters, but this was not the strategy taken. We don't permanently close a motorway when there's a car accident. Yet shuttering bars and music venues is often seen as the best solution to tackling antisocial behaviour. As Andrea Baker writes, by 2010 it was discovered that there were a number of "bizarre licence restrictions" on music venues in Yarra and Greater Melbourne.[10] The Tote was the next venue to give up.

The issues in Melbourne that affected these music venues were, as in many other cities, not specifically tied to music. Instead, the issues were related to alcohol, antisocial behaviour, gentrification, inflation and the increased cost of living that, over time, led to the prioritising of certain beliefs over others, or certain uses of land over others. When there are increased incidents of antisocial behaviour, it's easier to blame the places people congregate in, or places perceived to be full of drunks. The complex causes and symptoms of these issues, which include poverty, lack of education, structural racism, personal dissatisfaction, mental health care and issues of self-worth, are ignored. These are issues that require policies that include music and the measuring of music ecosystems. Closing a music venue and declaring the problem solved is much simpler. In many places, they are not specifically targeted, but in the case of the Tote and others in Melbourne at the time, it was argued (by a government seeking re-election) that if those specific venues did not exist, then antisocial behaviour and alcohol-fuelled violence wouldn't either. Many believed them.

Four years later, this was manifested in Sydney's Kings Cross area and greater Central Business District (CBD), when stringent licensing restrictions on bars and nightclubs, referred to as the "lockout laws", were passed. This decision was made by the state government and opposed by the city government, made possible because alcohol legislation sat at the state level, not at the city level. It was modelled on a similar law in the region of Newcastle, which saw a near 40% drop in assaults due to stricter licensing rules and a curfew.[11] In Sydney, the law prohibited bars from allowing new patrons in after 1.30am and imposed a strict 3am curfew. Research found that, while assaults dropped by 4% in the CBD and 53% in the Kings Cross neighbourhood, they increased elsewhere, with new nightlife areas experiencing a 30% increase in antisocial behaviour.[12] These laws sparked similar protests to the SLAM campaign in Melbourne and were said to have cost the city $16.1bn AUD in lost economic output,[13] before being repealed on 14 January 2020.

The protest in Melbourne also worked. Successive left and right governments no longer took live music for granted, and from the nadir of 2010 to the new nadir of 2021, more than $40m was invested into the contemporary music sector, and progressive planning and liquor licensing reforms were presented by industry and ushered through.

Soon after the SLAM Rally in 2010, Helen and her partner Quincy joined the live music roundtable, advising on how to reform music policies to better support the music ecosystem. Helen was later appointed to the Creative State Arts Advisory Panel. Paddy quit his job as the editor of *The Age* and was later appointed CEO of a new public funded body, Music Victoria, representing the industry's voice on numerous government boards and committees to ensure the music sector's voice was represented and that it was no longer the victim of unintended consequences. By 2014, through the collaboration of those that initiated SLAM, the Fair Go for Live Music collective and Music Victoria, it had implemented more progressive legislation to support and defend its music infrastructure. The Tote survived and remains open, albeit under new ownership. Melbourne, significantly impacted by the closures and challenges of the COVID pandemic is changing, but the regulations that govern live music have stayed the test of time. The city now faces new challenges, including fairly paying those who work in venues and addressing sexual based violence. Sydney, on the other hand, has appointed a 24 hour commissioner, Michael Rodrigues, and has reformed its regulations, which Marcou AM believes are challenging Melbourne's mantle in better supporting the music economy.[14] Melbourne, before the pandemic, claimed to have more music venues than any other city in the world, with one venue per 9,503 residents. London, by comparison, when measured, had one for every 34,350 residents. More venues does not mean a system is thriving and these headlines, in some ways, fuelled complacency, rather than action.

However, the Tote remains, and it is important to note that is the case because it is protected from encroachment by the Agent of Change law introduced in 2014, for which Paddy, Helen and many others from the music lobby advocated. This rule, a planning instrument not specifically related to music, ensured that the Tote, as well as other venues in Melbourne, were recognised across the city's wider land-use plan. This is important and something we'll look at later, as it has had profound impacts in other places, like London.

Changing Landscapes

Between 2005 and 2015, London lost about a third of its small- to medium-sized music venues.[15] Similar venue losses have occurred in other UK cities, including Sheffield, Bristol and Birmingham. In Seattle, half a dozen venues closed in the last five years, with even more under threat from the COVID-19 pandemic, inflation and the increased cost of living. The *New York Observer* cited eight landmark venues the city has lost since 2014, including the Roseland Ballroom.[16] Toronto has seen more than ten venues close since 2015.[17] In Vancouver, a loss of rehearsal spaces is a problem.[18] You might argue this is just part of the ever-changing ecosystem that is our cities — businesses open, businesses close — but the net rate of companies closing whose primary business is music shows a sharp increase since 2005, without including the negative impacts of the pandemic. Some of this is inevitable in the context of the music industry's recent economic history. Music sales halved in the 2000s, buoyed by the rise in illegal downloading.[19] The sector declined from \$14.6bn in 2000 to \$6.97bn in 2014, prompting a percentage of service businesses — venues, studios, rehearsal spaces — to follow suit.[20]

However, since 2014, the music business has regained its footing, and is now worth \$26bn annually, with a projected growth (prior to the pandemic) of reaching \$41bn by 2030, according to Goldman Sachs.[21] Music rights and the recorded sector continue to grow, with the International Federation of Phonographic Industries noting an 18.4% growth from 2021 to 2022,[22] despite the widespread closure of live music, festivals and their supply chains.[23] Former Chief Economist for Spotify, Will Page, argues music copyright alone is worth \$32.5bn.[24] However, the infrastructure, spaces, places and organisations set up to support the music industry around the world has not kept pace with the rise of streaming, Web3 or other advancements. The way we consume music is changing. Millions of us put headphones in and stream music via Spotify, Amazon, Deezer, Tidal or Apple Music and occasionally go to a concert. There was an interesting debate from the *Guardian* in 2018, which remarked:

> Spotify speaks to this silent majority of music fans. Audiophiles, object fetishists, anti-capitalists, musicians — these groups noisily protest Spotify, but are marginal compared with the number of ordinary listeners, who never read the liner notes in the first place. For many people, music is just for mood, something to work, exercise or have sex to — situations that Spotify usefully caters to with playlists such as Productive Morning, Extreme Metal Workout and 90s Baby Makers.[25]

More passive music listeners are good for the recorded music business. The more music that's heard, regardless of the context, the more revenue is generated for rights holders and performers. This goes beyond music. White noise, as an industry, is worth millions. A single playlist dedicated to white noise on Spotify earned an estimated $2.5m in revenue in 2021.[26] Two minutes of rainfall generated over 2 million streams. As a result, our relationship with music is changing. On average, we listen to between two and four hours per day, but most of the time we have no idea we're doing it.[27] Overall, we listen to more music than ever before,[28] yet this growth of the music business has happened alongside venue closures and, after a spike, a decline in live music takings. The live music business in the UK shrank in 2017. In China alone, it declined by 18% in 2018.[29] COVID-19 has exacerbated this — live music may take a decade to recover, and the early statistics are encouraging, with tickets up 10% on 2019 totals, according to Live Nation and Ticketmaster.[30] However, this hasn't been replicated with a 10% increase in teaching the tools of the trade to produce these gigs. The make-up of the music ecosystem, and who is winning and losing in it, is changing.

At the same time, there's significant growth in what's called "the experience economy" — paying to do stuff rather than paying to have stuff. According to the World Economic Forum, 78% of millennials prefer shelling out for experiences than for material possessions.[31] This furthers the contradiction that music inhabits: although the sector is expected to show net growth over the next decade, the infrastructure needed to facilitate experiences is in decline. More music is being consumed passively or in isolation. And because venues shuttered due to the pandemic, this furthers music becoming even more personal and less communal. Yes, we are going to more gigs now, but that may change as we emerge post-pandemic, facing a cost of living crisis. At the same time, the infrastructure needed to support such growth, should it continue to happen, is not everywhere. What this means for cities, especially those that lost small music venues and other spaces since 2019 is significant.

This is why we need to clearly separate the music industry from urban music ecosystems. Being concerned with the music ecosystem means more than labels, publishers and promoters, while still recognising that the growth in music everywhere benefits everyone who makes, trades and lives off of it. However, there are aspects of the ecosystem that have little in common with the objectives of the commercial music industry. Designing a public square so it can host buskers in a way that doesn't infuriate neighbours is not a primary concern for the commercial, rights-based recorded music business. More music is welcome, as rights revenue would be accrued, but if the square was silent, it wouldn't affect multinational record label's bottom lines. It is appreciated, but not necessary. The same goes for providing universal music education. That would lead to a larger talent pool, but with fewer artists earning the majority of revenue in the business; there's an argument that no matter what, great talent would find its way to the top. The holistic benefits of music to mental health or communities is welcome, and we would notice if it wasn't available for exercise or dementia care, but those outputs do not directly contribute to increased album or single sales. If they did, SoulCycle would have a record label.

That the music industry earns its keep in ways not wholly dependent on creating a music ecosystem that works for everyone has become more evident during the pandemic, where some sectors of the industry — record labels, publishers and streaming providers — continue to grow, while others — venues, festivals and emerging musicians — have struggled. Even during a pandemic, parts of the industry were in growth despite music education being reduced, and increasingly we value music based on singular tracks, artists or initiatives. If Ed Sheeran is responsible for nine of the top ten streamed tracks in the world, as he was in 2017, creating more revenue for the business because more people are streaming his music, this is seen as a success. Taylor Swift's tracks filled the Billboard top ten in October 2022, the first time one artist has ever done that. But this is only a success for Ed Sheeran, Taylor Swift and their teams, not for the music ecosystem as a whole.[32]

There is no music ecosystem policy of note at any level in Suffolk, where Sheeran lives, and while we celebrate his success, little is said of the years he played for free, busked on the streets (via policies that allowed him to do so) or toiled in grassroots music venues. He himself has spoken about it, but in the context of his success, this necessary step is often not mentioned as the stepping stone that it is. A smaller number of artists dominating the industry in fact demonstrates the exact opposite of the optimization of a music ecosystem, and while Sheeran or Swift may be celebrated for their economic impact, their success is not translated into a policy shift in the UK or US that mandates and funds music education, or reduces the tax burden on music venues, or ensure recording facilities are provided in community centres up and down the country.

Small music venues in north London pay higher property taxes per capita than the Emirates Stadium (where Arsenal Football Club play), for example. The Lexington, a 220-capacity venue in north London, saw its bill increase 118% in November 2017, while the Emirates' tax was cut 7% due to the inequity in the way taxes are measured.[33] It took three years, in early 2020, for the government to offer a 50% rate reduction for small music venues, which included the Lexington.[34]

To look at the issue from a different angle, in 1995, the average age of a Glastonbury headliner was 29. In 2015, it was 43.[35] In 2022, it was 45, rising to 48 if one does not include Billie Eilish and Kendrick Lamar.[36] Fewer artists achieving this kind of level of popularity creates another paradox: we all crave music, but lacking the mechanisms to invest in it, we get less choice because of the choices we are already making. While more music is being made and released than ever before, the amount we listen to, en masse, is shrinking. 90% of streaming revenue goes to the top 1% of artists.[37] This is for a variety of reasons. Many playlists are pay-to-play and algorithms are designed to give you more of what you like, rather than introduce you to something from a different genre. They are also rigged to introduce artists from the same label or publisher, depending on the advertising arrangements. As the music industry grows, it can be imagined like an hourglass — more value is accrued at the top, the pipeline compresses in the middle and squeezes and enlarges the bottom at the same time. This may not matter on a case-by-case basis, but it matters over time. Fewer artists releasing music that has less longevity drains the well. At some point, it could go dry.

This is further emphasised by where the money is in live music. The majority of growth, especially as the pandemic has eased, is in arenas, stadiums and large venues. Maybe we want to be outside more where we feel it's safer, or listen to music that is familiar to us, but this growth, according to economist Will Page, means stadiums, festivals and arenas have grown to represent 40% of the UK's live music market share, up from 23% in 2012.[38] This is great at the top of the hourglass, but more difficult for those below.

What's needed then is to move on from thinking about specific issues and artists to focusing on music as an ecosystem. This is the project that a small but growing number of people have been focusing on since the mid-2010s, and it is something that has defined my own life since 2015. This is the process and drive to create a different vision of "Music Cities" — cities that deliberately and intentionally, in one way or another, invest in, measure and analyse music. But being a Music City may not mean that it has a thriving music ecosystem. To better understand this, let's go back to the beginning and take a swerve into a more autobiographical view of the situation, exploring my experiments in creating Music Cities policies.

CHAPTER 3
LESSONS FROM THE STAGE

In January 2016, I was invited to join a music industry ski trip to Leysin, Switzerland, jokingly titled Music Think Ski. At that point, although the words "Music Cities" had appeared in some articles, little collective thought had been established, but this was slowly changing. In June 2015, the first Music Cities report not specific to any city was released, *The Mastering of a Music City*, led by Canada's major record label trade association Music Canada and the IFPI, the global record label lobby. That October, the Mayor of London's Music Venues Taskforce released a report to analyse the closure of a number of high-profile music venues and propose steps to address them. This is the report that itemised how many venues had closed between 2005-2015, as I mentioned earlier.

Music Cities was a topic that was of interest to many in the music industry, but that was it. Austin and Nashville were Music Cities. Melbourne was a Music City. New Orleans was a Music City. Those tags were assumed and not questioned. Nothing was invented in 2015 — as we've already discussed, the term "Nashville Music City" had been trademarked by the Nashville Visitors and Convention Bureau since 2007.[1] In 2004, a music policy conference was held in New Orleans by the Responsible Hospitality Institute, a night-time economy advocacy group, the first conference of its kind. The City of Chicago, in partnership with the University of Chicago, published a music strategy in 2007.[2] Toronto and Austin formed a Music Cities Alliance in 2013, which led to the development of the aforementioned *The Mastering of a Music City*.

The man behind the idea to create Musik Think Ski, Martin Elbourne, was hired by the South Australian Provincial Government to write a live music strategy for Adelaide and its surrounding region in 2013. Elbourne had spent three decades booking stages at Glastonbury and was a serial entrepreneur, launching festivals around the world, including the Great Escape in Brighton, England. His job was to work out how to support the development of live music in the region. The central business district of the city tended to empty at 6pm, and those working in the centre decamped to the suburbs. There was little to no live music economy. His report was expected to address this.

Many of the challenges noted in the report were alcohol-related, criticising decades-old laws. Licensing restrictions in South Australia were archaic and not designed to recognise, support and manage live music, similar to Victoria and New South Wales. The role of music was not mentioned in the laws, so the link between music and alcohol was left to interpretation, most often creating more restrictions for music. The regulations had no understanding of their role in supporting Adelaide's music ecosystem. This is common around the world. For example, it took until June 2022 for Rowan County, a rural county in Eastern Kentucky, United States, to allow for the sale of alcohol.[3] It was considered a dry county, an anachronistic regulation originating from nearly a century ago. There are still around 80 dry counties across nine states, which prohibit the sale of alcohol and with it any other business activity that happens when alcohol is served, including live music.[4] Prohibiting alcohol, or highly restricting it in the case of Adelaide, brings ancillary consequences, one of which is to heavily restrict the ability to stage live music, much as what happened in

Melbourne in 2010. Once again, music is impacted by a law that is meant to restrict something else.

For example, the Adelaide report states:

> Currently liquor licences can be granted, with conditions on the type of entertainment that is provided including the specification of the genres of music (for example, folk music or acoustic music only or "no grunge music"), or types of bands (for example, only solo acts, duets or two-piece bands). These restrictions are often imposed with the agreement of both parties but this is generally because the licensee wishes to avoid further cost.[5]

Due to these discriminatory conditions, certain genres of music were in effect prohibited from being performed live in the central business district. Light jazz? No problem! Metalcore? We have a problem! This is illustrative of how many cities approach live music, with planning and licensing laws not recognising the diversity of populations. When these laws were written, there was no metalcore, no hip-hop, no EDM and no grime. In many places, music wasn't yet electrified. While music changed, the law remained stationary. As a result, the music stopped in the central business district, and with it any viable evening or night-time economy and the jobs and revenues that come with it.

The report was released at the end of 2013. In its introduction, Martin essentially defined what Adelaide's music ecosystem could be, if the recommendations were adopted:

> A strong theme in this report is the need for a focus on the broader music industry and providing an infrastructure for its growth. This generally means providing the means for the development of various vocations and businesses.

There are many possible pathways to working in a music profession or vocation in South Australia but parts of the pathway are not readily available or always obvious. Specifically artists and music industry professionals who are in the mid stage of their careers do not necessarily have access to guidance and support that is required for them to move to the next step in their careers. Providing access to mentoring and to promotion of music products in national and international markets is likely to facilitate the advancement and growth of artists and other music careers alike. The development of skills and fostering creativity in future artists from an early age and ongoing is important to the state's capacity to produce successful artists as well as audiences on an ongoing basis.[6]

Its 47 recommendations addressed many of these inequities. By the end of 2015, Adelaide was seeing some successes by implementing the recommendations, although some of the momentum stalled due to a change of government in 2018 and the impact of the pandemic. A new organisation, Musitec, was set up to deliver them and a creative hub was established in an abandoned church. All of this was happening before we hit the slopes in January 2016.

The trip was the idea of Martin and Marc Ridet, who has a long history of managing bands and at the time managed the Swiss music export office — a sort of trade office to promote music — for the French-speaking part of Switzerland. Both love to ski. Armed with a discounted rate from a chalet owned by friends of Marc and free lift passes courtesy of the local authority, Marc and Martin set out to create a new music industry mini-conference, and the concept of Music Cities was one of the topics of discussion.

All of us worked full-time in the commercial music industry, across record labels, festivals, venues, music publishers and artist management, but few of us had an understanding of planning, building codes, noise ordinances, landscaping, soundscaping, health and social care policy, music education policy or how city councils operate or allocate budgets. The people in the room knew how to book artists, promote concerts, manage bands and make money with music, and our ideas of Music Cities were based on creating cities with thriving music industries. At the time, that included protecting and preserving music venues in London, developing more live music in Adelaide or (in my own case) promoting the positive impact of export offices, be it representing Canadian bands or those from other countries, which is what I was doing at the time as a sort of export office for hire which is what my company, Sound Diplomacy, offered as a service.

Turning from Music Export to Music Cities

In February of 2015, then-Mayor of London Boris Johnson announced that his culture team was creating a Music Venues Taskforce to investigate why so many music venues in London were closing down. I wanted to get involved as the first venue I went to when I moved to London, the Luminaire, had shut down, as had Turnmills in Farringdon and the Astoria in Tottenham Court Road, also venues I had seen shows at. I was a concerned citizen who wanted to help, so I reached out to the Mayor's Office and offered my support, but as I had no expertise in policies related to cities and music venues, there was no reason for anyone to respond. At the same time, Martin's report was being implemented, which provided the opportunity to try to sell it to other cities, and so he approached me about the idea of Music Cities and turning this report — a concept with some recommendations — into a product.

Over the first half of 2015, this is what we attempted, reaching out to 30 or so friends and colleagues in a number of cities around the world. No one understood why they should pay to have a music policy written for them for a number of reasons:

"Music doesn't need help."

"There's live music everywhere."

"Music is inherently anti-establishment, so it should be kept away from the government."

"This is something the music industry should do, as they are the only ones that benefit."

"I don't like that type of music that's becoming popular, so I'm not going to support it."

"We're a city of arts or theatre."

"We'd love to become a Music City, but we don't want to spend any money to make it happen."

Suffice to say, we were unsuccessful.

Having hit a wall, we tried another tactic — approaching London property developers. Near our office in Shoreditch at the time, there was a development — now a district where people live and work — called the Stage. Built on the site of Shakespeare's original theatre, the Stage is mixed-use, meaning its plans included housing, retail, performance and ancillary space. Its marketing pack said a new theatre was going to be developed there. I researched the development's head of marketing and gave them a call. Maybe the theatre could double as a music venue, and I thought I knew how to make that happen. The conversation went something like this:

"Sorry, who are you?"

"My name is Shain and I want to talk to you about Music Cities."

"Sorry, what are Music Cities?"

"Um, well, have you thought of the role of music at the Stage."

"Well, that's up to each individual tenant. They can play whatever music they like."

"No, I mean…"

"Sorry, I have a meeting."

She hung up.

The next day I decamped with Martin and one of my board members at Sound Diplomacy, Rob, to a pub. I told them how I had embarrassed myself over the phone and that we would never be hired by a developer to do anything because we didn't know what the hell we're doing. Yes, everyone wanted a thriving music scene in their city, but everyone had venues, festivals and artists, hence nothing was wrong. The problem wasn't being articulated, all cities already thought of themselves as Music Cities. It was also too early for any of the recommendations in the Adelaide report to be enacted, nor did we have a mechanism to track what would or would not happen in Adelaide. The report was an academic initiative commissioned by a foundation aligned with an academic institution; outline the issues, posit a hypothesis, review existing literature and study, wait and report. Any immediate action would have to be evaluated in the future, and as we didn't have a successful use case, the question had been asked but no answers existed yet.

As I have already mentioned, the place that was coming closest to answering these questions — particularly what the concept of Music Cities meant — was in fact in my own backyard. The Mayor's Office in London had established a Music Venues Taskforce in February 2015, so we hatched a plan. Through the Great Escape Festival in Brighton, which was and remains the largest urban music business conference and showcasing event in the UK, Martin already had relationships with venues, caterers, production companies, marketing firms and the city council. There was no event happening the day before the event started, Wednesday 18 May, and we thought, if everyone was ignoring us, we would need to do better at explaining what we were arguing needed to be done in cities. We also thought that, by forcing a conversation, something half-decent would emerge from it that we could use to sell our wares. If we promised to feed people, we knew they would spend the day with us, especially because our potential audience and initial clientele was coming to the Great Escape anyways. If we filled the day with friends discussing things they were doing around the world, they'd come because they were speaking, and most importantly, if there was enough interest we could persuade the Mayor's Office in London to jump on a train and come to Brighton.

The Music Cities Convention

On 8 February 2015, we announced the Music Cities Convention. The idea was to promote Martin's report, welcome the authors of the Canadian Music Cities report —

The Mastering of a Music City — to present their initial findings, and most importantly, convince the Mayor's Office to let me join the task force. Our tagline was "Music Makes Cities Better". There are hundreds of music conferences around the world, and we were conscious to try and offer different programming. Our goal was for the programming to not be about one's particular music or craft, but about the impact their actions delivered for their community and how it could be replicated, and so we didn't want to stack the deck with music industry speakers, each proclaiming how important they were to their respective cities.

Instead, we asked our friends to present about the cities they work in, drawing on a line-up of people attending the Great Escape already, ultimately featuring speakers from Toronto, Addis Ababa, Adelaide (of course), London and Berlin. No one came to speak at the conference without already planning to come to the Great Escape. The speakers were who we knew, and we even enticed Dave Haslam, author and former Hacienda DJ, to speak. The City of Manchester, however, wasn't present, nor we did not have one Mayor or Chief of Staff speak, no heads of economic development or heads of tourism. There were no chambers of commerce, local enterprise partnerships, economic development councils or community development foundations. We didn't invite them as we didn't know how. Two weeks before the event, we had sold eight tickets, and undoubtedly a few speakers had bought them out of pity. Over the final two weeks, a further 40 tickets were sold and we gave the rest away, allowing us to claim that we had sold out the Music Cities Convention, which luckily enticed the London Mayor's Office to take a risk and show up.

The event was to run from 10am-6pm with the promise to vacate by 6:30pm, as we were using the Komedia, a movie theatre that had scheduled to show *The Avengers* at

7pm. There was no urban planning or regeneration policy in the program. The word "ordinance" wasn't mentioned, nor were tax incentives, enterprise areas or heads-in-beds tax discussed. It was a communal, friendly meeting of minds to reaffirm something we all agreed on — that music has a value which is bigger than our independent work within it. In addition to the value of music to our industry, a groupthink exercise was started, with 120 people exploring what the value of music meant in regard to where they lived and their built environment.

Back to the Taskforce

London had a music venue closure problem. The Astoria shut due to the construction of east-west rail link Crossrail, now called the Elizabeth Line. Earl's Court closed in 2014, due to redevelopment of the area into a new housing neighbourhood, although new venues are returning to the area, at Olympia and, in a few years' time, Earl's Court as well. The Marquee Club closed in 2012. Turnmills, a famous nightclub in Farringdon, closed in 2008. Metro, whose indie nights soundtracked my weekends when I first moved to London, played its last record in 2009. The Luminaire, the first venue I saw a gig in London in Kilburn shut its doors to become apartments. In total, over 45 venues disappeared from 2007 to 2015, prompting the Mayor of London's Culture Team to assemble the Music Venues Taskforce. Interviewed in *Time Out* on 4 June, then-Mayor of London Boris Johnson stated:

I am as concerned as any music-lover about the threat to live music venues and have set up a Live Music Taskforce [sic], which has been talking to musicians, venues and local government with the aim of developing a practical plan of action to ensure live music in all its forms is integrated into our city's future growth. It's due to release a first report this summer.[7]

The Music Venues Taskforce consisted of industry trade associations, music venues owners and the Mayor's Office. London has one of the world's largest clusters of music industry jobs and houses Europe's largest music industry. All the major labels have offices in the city. Live Nation's European headquarters is there, as are AEG's and venue-builder Oakview Group and digitial service provider Spotify. Many global superstars were managed by Londoners. But despite this, venues were still closing and there was seemingly no correlation between a healthy music industry and a thriving music ecosystem. Consolidation was protecting venues owned by multinationals, but grassroots or independently owned or operated music venues were struggling. There are many reasons for this, some of which are not specific to the individual venues themselves, such as the increase in land value across London and changing tastes, but essentially a thriving music industry controlled by large multinational corporations does not mean that music venues thrive, nor does it mean music education is protected, that cities have progressive street performance and noise and building code policies that support music-makers and businesses.

The Music Venues Taskforce report, *London's Grassroots Music Venue Rescue Plan*, was principally written by the Mayor's music lead Paul Broadhurst — the guy I bothered enough to convince to come to Music Cities Convention — and Mark Davyd, who led the Music Venue Trust, along with his wife and co-conspirator Beverley Whitrick, and led the fight to save grassroots music venues in the UK. I assisted in the research and editing of the report, and contributed a quote. The objective was to move the ownership of land that small- and medium-sized venues sat on into a trust, so their use could be protected regardless of who held the lease. Without such protection, music venues were subject to the vagaries of the rental or development market — a supermarket or block of flats could produce more yield for the landowner than a venue. The charity has since created a lease-holding firm, Music Venue Properties, and is selling shares in it to punters and fans alike, to buy the land underneath venues and protect them as such.

The report was released in October 2015, a few months later than Boris Johnson had promised, and it boldly showed that music venues in the city needed a rescue plan. The press around the launch was astounding. From the headline, "Boris Johnson backs Frank Turner led campaign"[8] to "Music industry won't find stars of tomorrow without radical change", it made public the stark reality London was facing.[9] 35% of small-to-medium-sized music venues had closed down. No one knew what the statistics were for recording studios, but it was assumed it was similar. In 2007, London had 135 of these venues, but by 2015 only 88 were left, with many others threatened with closure.

For the first time, the Mayor of London's administration outlined a policy objective related to a specific issue in the music ecosystem, other than stating that music was important and letting it be governed by other policies. A problem was identified and a set of solutions, all contained in the report, were presented; what was needed was a coordinated effort to enact these solutions.

The report's recommendations were quickly being adopted. The creation of a Night Time Commission and a separate London music board was announced, the goal of which was to decide if London should appoint a Night Mayor — a policy position to advise and work on issues related to the night-time economy. These roles had been in place in Belgium, Switzerland, the Netherlands and Germany for years.

It seemed that London's emerging music policy work had taken off. When the next mayoral election happened in April 2016, Sadiq Khan, a Labour politician, won. His campaign manifesto included a number of provisions linked to the *Grassroots Music Venues Rescue Plan*, and throughout the spring and summer of 2016, both the London Music Board and the Night Time Commission met. The London Music Board brought together organisations from across London to develop consensus on how to enact more recommendations of the *Rescue Plan*. The Night Time Commission, in its first incarnation, had a specific objective: it supported an external report to quantify the value of London's night-time economy and get agreement to appoint a Night Mayor. The position's title was changed to Night Czar and a recruitment process began. The London Music Board continued to grow at the time, hosting between 20-30 representatives at City Hall every two months.

Then the UK voted for Brexit, which, while it did not change the nature of the work, made clear that budgets would have to be reallocated to Brexit preparations across London. Additionally, many of the policy amendments required to support music venues in London had nothing to do with music directly, so rather than lobbying for more support for London's music industry, the answer was to develop strategies to convince the police, private developers and local councillors that music mattered to them. This is what led to the first major collective success — changing England's planning laws.

It was patently obvious that the way planning law was interpreted, implemented and governed was one of the reasons why venues were closing at an accelerating pace. In 2015, in an effort to fast-track housebuilding, the UK government tweaked the planning rules to create the "permitted development rights" framework. Permitted development rights impact all manner of land uses and, in many respects, allow for changes in how land is used without going through planning permission, which takes time and money. In this case, the changes allowed offices to be converted into residential premises, without seeking full planning approvals. Much of these conversions happened in business parks and have led to homes being created out of office blocks. According to the *Guardian* journalist Oliver Wainwright:

> After studying hundreds of new homes carved out from converted offices, shops, warehouses and industrial buildings, created between 2015 and 2018 through permitted development, a team of academics from University College London and the University of Liverpool found predictably grim results. The planning loophole had unleashed a new breed of tiny, dingy apartments, many barely fit for human habitation, with rooms accessed from long corridors, windows looking across internal atriums into other people's rooms, and some bedrooms with no windows at all.[10]

In addition, offices above pubs were converted to housing, with no additional soundproofing, and on high streets housing developments emerged where there were once offices and commercial premises. As these developments were built, sold and inhabited, a number of issues became apparent. When residents can't sleep due to pounding bass, single-glazed windows or the dispersal of a nightclub across the street at 4am, tensions rise, noise complaints increase and venues are blamed.

A high-profile example of this was Ministry of Sound, a nightclub in south London. Ministry of Sound welcomes 2,000-3,000 clubbers every weekend, but in 2011 a housing application to develop new tower blocks in front of the venue was submitted.[11] The club, concerned about the threat to its licence due to noise complaints, launched a legal challenge that cost it over £1m to fight. In the end, the club and the developer agreed to a "deed of easement", which requires the people buying the properties to recognise, in their contracts, the existence of the nightclub and forgo their right to complain about its business, so long as Ministry of Sound follows its licensing protocol. Similar agreements have been made in other parts of the country, including with the Stables in Milton Keynes and the George Tavern in East London, but these are exceptions, rather than the norm. Overwhelmingly, permitted development rights accelerated the closures of music venues in London and the UK. It became a choice — homes or culture — with few people arguing that in fact they're mutually beneficial. These sorts of conflicts can often be avoided through conversation, negotiation, communication and careful, long-term planning, but in London at the time, there was no one to lead the conversation with authority and influence. Solving this was the objective of the Night Czar position, filled by nightclub promoter Amy Lamé in November 2016.

I had been consulting with the Mayor's Office since September 2015, having been hired after the success of the Music Cities Convention. Pleading with the Mayor of London's culture team to come to Brighton worked. My team and I acted as the secretariat of the London Music Board and Night Time Commission, worked on the recruitment process of the Night Czar and helped draft minutes, reports and evidence to further the recommendations of the taskforce. I was spending half my week at City Hall, with a municipal email address and a remit of supporting the development of London's music policy. At the same time, Sound Diplomacy's work was changing from working on music export to working with cities, aided by these contracts to work at City Hall. By November and December 2016, it was time to produce an update on the work supporting music venues, and *Making Progress: Grassroots Music Venues*

Rescue Plan Update was published in 2017 and launched at the Social, a small grassroots music venue behind Oxford Street in central London. The key finding was that venue closures had stabilised in London. What was being done, in some regard, was working. While venues had closed over the 18 months since the initial report was written, new venues had also opened. In addition, the Mayor committed to enacting the Agent of Change principle in the London Plan, the governing land-use plan for the city, as recommended in the first *Grassroots Music Venues Rescue Plan*. This was a landmark decision, because it would reverse the problems caused by permitted development rights.

The Agent of Change principle is one of the simplest mechanisms available to better understand how a mix of uses — residential, commercial, entertainment — can be planned effectively, if it is incorporated into all land-use decisions and conscientiously used. The principle, which originated in Australia and was key in the case of the Tote, has also been utilised by the San Francisco Entertainment Commission in its dense urban core since 2003. It requires that the agent creating the change — be it a developer or investor — mitigate the impact of the change on its neighbours, usually within a few hundred square feet of the development. In the simplest terms, if a new block of flats is planned next to an existing bar or music venue, it is the developer of the flats' responsibility to soundproof effectively or design accordingly (such as not having single-glazed windows or balconies facing the action), and the same goes for one interested in building a venue in a residential neighbourhood or refitting an industrial space.

The Agent of Change principle is not unique to music and noise — it also governs where industrial uses can be permitted next to housing developments, or how many charity or betting shops can be in any town centre. The objective is to avoid conflict through the planning system, so neighbours can in fact be neighbourly. This rule, committed to the London Plan first and then incorporated into the National Planning Policy Framework (NPPF) six months later, was not a panacea, but it was a statement of intent. Filtering down to planning committees and development proposals, it required developers to know what was around them and to plan accordingly when entertainment and culture were involved. After being incorporated into law in England, it was implemented in Wales, Scotland and Northern Ireland, becoming the first Agent of Change requirement incorporated into an entire national planning framework.

In the 18 months from May 2015 to January 2017, with the Agent of Change principle enacted in London (and soon to be replicated nationwide), a Night Czar in office and a functioning London Music Board and Night Time Commission in situ, the concept of Music Cities was a reality and my work, which began with being hung up on by a developer, had changed. I was now engaged full-time in Music Cities work. London offered a very high-profile case study where a problem was identified and solutions were mapped out and executed. Not everything was successful — venues still closed and, in many regards, grassroots music venues were over-prioritised, ignoring an equally pressing challenge facing recording studios, rehearsal spaces and music education programs. But the value that music brought to London, to its built environment, was better qualified and quantified. The role of local policymakers, in contributing to how music — as an ecosystem — could be governed in a city, was being beta tested.

But the closure of music venues is not the only problem impacting music ecosystems. It can be far more pernicious. One issue that became apparent, as our work with cities developed and I began to travel around the world to work with municipalities, was systemic racism. Music, as something that can be enjoyed and experienced by everyone, is often not available in the same way to everyone in all communities around the world. This is an issue that, in many places, is poorly addressed. But when it is taken on, and improved, it can be a powerful tool in community empowerment as a whole. This is best told through another city with which I have worked — Madison, the capital of Wisconsin in America, where, unlike most places, the community addressed systemic racism in music head on.

Challenging Systemic Racism: Madison, Wisconsin

In 2018, the city of Madison, Wisconsin, commissioned two academics to produce a report outlining racial inequity in the city's music ecosystem.[12] The report, issued as part of an initiative called the Music and Equity Taskforce, was meant to make recommendations to the Mayor and the Common Council to improve upon Madison's reputation as a music and entertainment hub that offers an enjoyable and welcoming environment for all of its residents and guests of all ages, thereby providing positive social, cultural, and economic impact for Madison.[13]

The findings were shocking. Madison was described as "a mid-sized city that prides itself on beautiful lakes and rich arts and culture offerings. Yet, while Madison has often topped lists of 'most liveable' cities, it has also topped lists as the worst place to live for Black citizens."[14]

The report continued:

It may not come as a surprise that root cause analysis conducted by this task force indicated that the number one barrier to maintaining diverse entertainment catering to patrons of color is racism. Often the terms "urban" or "Hip-

Hop" are used as code to refer to events or circumstances that involve groups of Black people or other people of color. This practice directly affects equity in music and entertainment as well as other parts of city life. Other related root causes include biased media coverage, lack of small- to mid-sized entertainment venues, lack of cultural understanding of Hip-Hop or other underrepresented music genres, and a difference in perception of artists associated with UW-Madison as compared to artists in the community at large. This leads to the false impression that these genres are equitably represented.[15]

In 1997, Madison welcomed a $50m philanthropic investment to build a concert hall, the Overture Center.[16] The city and the county it sits in invest heavily in arts and culture. Its median income is at nearly $67,000, higher than the US average of $56,000.[17] It has a long history of cultural philanthropy, both tied to academia (through the University of Wisconsin) and a number of local corporate donors. Its cultural representative, Karin Wolf, spoke at the first American Music Cities Convention in October 2015.

However, these investments and wealth did not benefit all residents. Instead, music was used as a tool to discriminate against Black and Brown residents, according to the Music and Equity Taskforce. The findings went on:

Community pressure has limited the increase of venue ownership by communities of color. Inclusion of hip-hop in some venues' programming is affected by community pressure. Negative perception has fueled resistance to hip-hop venues and shows within the city.

The academic who led the Taskforce was Dr Karen Reece, and community leaders, businesses and musicians expressed a desire to implement the Taskforce's 31 recommendations and move forward. These recommendations included the following:

1. Within one year, the City of Madison should create a full-time staff position in the Mayor's office at $60,000 per year (including pay and benefits) focused exclusively on promoting equity in arts and entertainment.
2. Within one year, the City of Madison should work with festival organizers who are receiving City funds to ensure that artists of color, and specifically Hip-Hop artists, are incorporated into their programming.
3. Within two years, all venues with an entertainment licence with more than 14 employees submit an Affirmative Action Plan similar to entities contracting or receiving grant money from the City of Madison. It should emphasize EEOC (Equal Employment Opportunities Commission) language and discrimination definitions when granting these licenses.
4. Within five years, Hip-Hop should be incorporated into all kinds of events, including those at licensed entertainment venues and publicly accessible events such as Taste of Madison and Art Fair on the Square.
5. Within five to ten years, the City of Madison should work to support a music festival featuring Hip-Hop music, dance, and visual arts, R&B, etc.[18]

The result was the creation of a new public/private initiative, Greater Madison Music City, and a financial commitment in October 2020 of around $40,000 — mostly derived from hotel tax receipts. A further $50,000 was provided via a grant through the National Endowment for the Arts.[19] In budget proposals for 2021, despite shortfalls due to the costs of managing the local COVID-19 pandemic, the city retained its pre-pandemic arts and culture budget. This is a living, breathing music ecosystem at work, grappling with its inequities, history and structural racism. Karen is one of many in the music ecosystem working to make, as they see it, Madison better. But Madison is not unique — it is one city of thousands that face similar challenges related to systemic racism, access to resources and structural inequity. However, in 2018, Madison decided to do something about it, and two years later, change began.[20]

While the pandemic has slowed Madison's progress, it has continued to develop a wider data set to explain the challenges facing Black and Brown musicians, and what could potentially be done about it. An op-ed in *Tone Madison*, the local alternative magazine, led with the headline: "Music in Madison can pay, if you're white and not a musician."[21] In Madison, according to the research, the average income for musicians and those engaged in the music sector is shown as $29,968 for white people, $13,485 for Black people, and $12,715 for Asian people. In the wider economy, the median income is $50,943 for white people, $31,867 for Black people, and $45,529 for Asian people.[22]

Convincing communities that reform is needed requires showing that structures and policies are fractured. The outpouring of protest in the wake of the murder of George Floyd in Minneapolis in June 2020 — an act that influenced Madison's accelerated work to implement the reforms of the Taskforce — has galvanised cities across the world. COVID-19 had the same effect. We can see that to understand a music ecosystem and initiate change within it, you must realise that music impacts much more than the act of performing or the joy of the experience. Limiting music limits humanity, access and opportunity. Madison had music deserts, where access to space and educational and performance opportunities was limited, simply due to where one lived and what one looked like. Madison took the step — one that remains fractious and slow, but still positive — to address these issues. Few cities have done this in such an upfront manner — state the problem and the privilege and make a plan to do something about it.

Here we have the beginnings of a new way of thinking about music as a tool to tackle the roots of structural racism in urban planning and quality of life, if explored through rewriting local policy. Lines have to be drawn to ensure that fairness, equity, inclusion and fact-based assessment criteria are assigned to all policies designed to support — or understand — music ecosystems. While every city, neighbourhood and recording studio is different, they are unified in the fact that music is prevalent. Some cities ignore it, choosing to let music remain a hobby or a form of entertainment, and some embrace it as a structural tool for making and remaking. Madison continues to do this through its Greater Madison Music City project, which has commissioned research to map the city's assets, better understand how to incorporate music into overall planning and continue community conversations.

Ground rules affect how we define music ecosystems and what goals, objectives and results we can expect from investing in them and building policies for them. In 2015, I would have said a music ecosystem working is the ability to buy tickets to a gig, attend safely and repeat the process as often as I wished. If artists were being discriminated against in Madison, that wouldn't have crossed my mind — it didn't affect me. Even if I lived in Madison, as a white, straight male, it would not have impacted me as much, or I may not have noticed it as I was blinded by my privilege. The music ecosystem that mattered to me was *my* music ecosystem. While I wished for everyone to have the same opportunities and access that I had, as long as gigs were on sale and I had the means to attend, all was right in the world.

Equally, as COVID-19 closed the live music business, how I experienced music changed, but my access to it remained. I switched to streaming. But that was predicated on high-speed Internet access and the disposable income to pay for it. I had both, so I was lucky. Many in Madison, and many other parts of the world, do not.

My music ecosystem was predicated on immediacy and efficiency. But in thinking this way, my music ecosystem was diverging from the reality of many others. Some were in freefall; others had disappeared. Many never existed in the first place. Now all musicians were unable to perform live. The inequity was extended past MCs and DJs to include guitarists, drummers and concert violinists. Those who never had high-speed Internet to stream music had more pressing priorities, including food and heat. But I could still listen to Phish on Spotify.

What has become clear — and what Karen and others in Madison realised — is that there's a convergence point where *my music ecosystem* and *other music ecosystems* intersect, which make the pain points and problems clearer. And if everyone's own music ecosystems are not considered, there is a problem. Spending $50m on a concert hall is a modest sum for a facility that can welcome the best classical, opera, ballet, jazz and live theatre with terrific sound, lights and facilities. Doing so without also investing in DJ booths, after-school programs and church choirs is counter-intuitive. It may not have been intentional, but it is what it is. When an entire music ecosystem across race, class, geography, gender and other lines is not considered, inequity prospers, and music, as a tool to support community cohesion and development, is in many places silenced.

An ecosystem must be made up of functioning parts. There is a holistic, universal understanding of what is required to build a functioning car — an engine, seats, a steering wheel. When exploring what an ideal or optimised music ecosystem is, this is less clear. Now is the time to establish clarity and learn from London, Madison, Melbourne and dozens of other cities around the world.

Back to Australia

In November 2020, the government of New South Wales in Australia passed a sweeping reform of live music policy.[23] A number of arcane laws existed similar to those in South Australia and Victoria, including prohibiting mirror balls in some venues and allowing certain bars to showcase only certain types of live music, or only being able to host concerts by cover bands. The *Guardian* described one small pub:

> For more than 30 years, the South Dubbo Tavern has been operating under bizarre conditions of a liquor licence that permitted only small cover bands to perform in the venue. The conditions meant the owner, Lee Green, could hire a trio of musicians performing Cold Chisel songs, but if Jimmy Barnes and his band were to show up at the Dubbo hotel, Green would be in breach of his licence if he allowed them to perform. "It says I'm allowed solos, duos, cover bands and country music bands, but no rock bands," Green said. "It doesn't make much sense to me... but then this [licensing agreement] was written in 1989... so yeah, you could say it's a bit outdated."[24]

This overhauling of policies that cross many government departments — culture, planning, licensing, economic development and others — is the most far-reaching reform ever implemented at once to support a live music ecosystem. Many of these rules, however outdated they were, were not known by the general public. Those abiding by them changed their business practices to comply, which cost money. No rock bands altered the manner in which Lee Green programmed his venue, but the impact of these regulations, built over many years and framed on trends, opinions, emotions and inconsistencies, destabilised the New South Wales live music sector. The COVID-19 pandemic made it worse, so much so that this opportunity for mass reform was offered. A policy that recognised live music as an ecosystem was realised. We should all take note. These reforms are specific to live music as its own ecosystem. But they provide a blueprint to think about what an ideal music policy could be and the impact it could have.

Last year, while sitting alone reading at Denver airport waiting for a delayed flight, Death Cab for Cutie's song "Gold Rush" came on the overhead PA at the airport bar. It was quiet enough not to disturb conversation, but loud enough so those who recognised the song were able to welcome it in their day. I began to lip-sync the words while reading, unconsciously splitting my attention between my book and the song. I popped my head up for a second and scanned the room. My eye caught a fellow traveller who looked as tired as me, also sipping a beer at the other side of the bar. She was also lip-syncing the words. We smiled at each other for a second, a unifying moment of togetherness at a time when I was immersed in solitude. But what if there were rules stating that the bar in Denver was only allowed to play disco or cover music? I know this sounds facetious, but these were the regulations for bars and pubs in New South Wales until November 2020.

The arguments made in New South Wales were both economic and based on reason — licensing conditions implemented in 1989, prior to the Internet, were anachronistic. Because of these regulations, built on top of each other like a bad Jenga game over 30 years, revenue was lost. When instituted, each had convinced legislators, regulators and publicans that they were logical, needed and for the greater good. The fact that it took the economic collapse of a sector due to a pandemic to determine that these regulations contributed little, and in many cases made things worse for those abiding by them, demonstrates how illogical they were. This mass change in policy had never happened before. Often laws are repealed or changed one at a time, rather than a package drawn up and changed in one fell swoop.

In addition, multiple government departments were involved in the reform. In creating a government, we separate policy areas into departments meant to manage singular affairs — this includes ministries responsible for tourism, housing, economic development and the economy. But the issues concerning live music incorporated each of these departments with no guidelines or joined-up thinking to bring them together. Who cares if only cover bands are allowed to perform, so long as the bar was able to sell alcohol? Not allowing original music had no bearing as to whether a planning application for housing would be approved next door. But each of these independent departments impacted the live music ecosystem, with no language to bring them together. The housing policy ecosystem clashed with the alcohol and liquor regulatory ecosystem, and music was caught in the middle. It was all single-issue politics.

Music is negatively impacted when treated by policy in this way. A singular policy to promote tourism, for example, could create a marketing campaign that forgets to pay artists for their music or to perform live. A skills policy to bolster music education may not be in sync with tax codes, hampering the ability for music and other cultural entrepreneurs to access capital. Yet it's the norm in most cities and places. When we look at single issues, the ability for music ecosystems to thrive as a cohesive whole, one that can be used to enhance a number of policy areas at once, is reduced.

So what is an example that can be learned from? To best explain, I want to take you to Huntsville, Alabama, where my team and I were commissioned to conduct a music audit, which was, at the time, the largest such project commissioned in the United States. After that, I'll propose a blueprint for music ecosystem policy that we can take forward, regardless of the city you're in.

CHAPTER 4
HUNTSVILLE

The Rocket City

After World War II, the United States transferred a number of German scientists to Fort Bliss, Texas, contracting them to work on military technology. One of them was Wernher von Braun, an astrophysicist who helped develop missile technology for the Nazis. He surrendered in 1944 and was relocated to the United States to work for the military. In 1950, von Braun was transferred to Huntsville to work at the Redstone Arsenal facility, a secret government compound on the outskirts of town dedicated to advanced defence technology.

Von Braun settled in Huntsville, likening it topographically to the hills in Germany where he grew up. And over the course of 20 years, he made a number of technological and cultural developments that have defined the north Alabama city ever since. As head of the United States Rocket Research Center, and later the Director of the Army Ballistic Missile Agency, von Braun led the American response to the space race with the Soviet Union, which launched its first rocket, Sputnik 2, in 1957. What followed effectively consolidated United States space technology development in Huntsville and with it, a bustling arts and cultural scene to support those who came to work at Redstone Arsenal. Von Braun was also instrumental in founding the Huntsville Symphony Orchestra and personally supported a number of art museums before eventually being transferred to Alexandria, Virginia, in 1970.

At roughly the same time — and by coincidence — in Muscle Shoals, 70 miles to the west, music producer Rick Hall established Florence Alabama Music Enterprises (FAME) in 1959. The Muscle Shoals region — made up of four separate towns: Florence, Sheffield, Muscle Shoals and Tuscumbia — became an incubator of music talent much like Redstone Arsenal was to engineering talent in the east. So while von Braun and his team developed missile and rocket technology to support the first space missions, Aretha Franklin, the Rolling Stones and scores of others were recording music at both FAME and nearby Muscle Shoals Sound Studios.

Huntsville, through the development projects occurring at Redstone Arsenal, became known for space, defence technology and missiles, not music. Redstone Arsenal is a place that few people know, but whose output we have all seen. The massive government worksite is home to a number of classified military and defence activities. Much of the nuts and bolts that support America's vast space program remain here, along with a tourist attraction, the Space and Rocket Center, to celebrate it, complete with a giant rocket in the parking lot. It is the busiest attraction in Alabama. To support the sector, thousands of companies that service the United States' military-industrial complex have Huntsville branches.

There are a number of ways cities invest in music, as we have discussed. Marketing campaigns to sell the destination is one such way. Owning and operating a landmark music venue is another. Employing city staff specifically to support the local music scene also happens. Developing and convening forums so musicians and businesses can interact and collaborate is one more tactic. Huntsville, the first time I visited, had few of these. Much of its economy was focused on science, engineering and maths, attracting those interested in technology and space exploration.

But like all cities, those who live here do not work 24 hours a day. They need something to do after work, or life is boring. Huntsville, like all cities, had a number of leisure facilities to support its residents: bowling alleys, cinemas, gyms, soft play areas, and outside the city limits, nature trails and hiking options for exploring the Tennessee Valley. The city also had a number of music assets, including a symphony orchestra, an opera company and its downtown venue, the Von Braun Center, which hosted concerts. There were recording studios and rehearsal spaces, and Oakwood University, the Historical Black University (HBCU) had developed a prestigious choir called The Aeoliens, which has been one of America's leading choirs since 1946, complimenting a robust and engaged music programme. There was music in Huntsville like there is everywhere. But music was not a strategic city priority. It existed for those who wished to participate in it. And with Nashville and Muscle Shoals both short drives away, it was not seen as worthy of intentional investment city wide, as one would expect, given it is sandwiched between two of America's most storied music communities. But I was wrong. Music was a priority for the city. This is what led to me sitting on the top floor of Huntsville City Hall in 2017, meeting with Mayor Tommy Battle and his team.

From Sofia to Huntsville

To understand what happened in Huntsville, we need to go back to a music conference in Sofia, Bulgaria, eight years earlier. The South Eastern European Music Event (SEEME) is one of dozens of mid-sized music conferences around Europe that I attended in my role as UK and

European Representative of the Canadian Independent Music Association, before I founded Sound Diplomacy. This was before Spotify, a time when you came away from conferences weighed down with a bag full of CDs. I was at SEEME to take part in a panel about music export and tactics to attract booking agents to work with emerging acts, and it was there I met Scott Cohen.

Scott founded the Orchard, one of the world's largest digital music distributors, now part of Sony Music. When I launched Sound Diplomacy in 2013, Scott became the Chairman, a position he held until the end of 2019.

As Sound Diplomacy pivoted from working on exporting artists to focus more on engaging cities, which began around the launch of the Music Cities Convention, we needed introductions to prospective clients, as those who would pay us were mainly organisations I did not know. By 2017, we had organised three Music Cities Conventions and I had been consulting with the London Mayor's Office for a little over a year, complete with London Music Board meetings and the creation of the Night Czar. It was Scott's network that led me to Huntsville. He introduced me to Drew Young, who at the time was music programs manager for the State of Mississippi, a public sector job that to this day only exists in a few places. Mississippi branded itself as the "Birthplace of American Music" and invested heavily in music tourism, including developing blues and country music trails and tourism initiatives. Not to mention, Mississippi is home to the birthplaces of B.B. King, Muddy Waters, Elvis Presley, and of course, Robert Johnson's famed crossroads. Drew was the link I needed. He introduced me to a property developer and philanthropist in Nashville named Aubrey Preston. Aubrey is one of a consortium of investors that bought RCA Studio A, along with former Senator Bill Frist and musician Ben Folds, in Nashville in order to save it from demolition. He also launched a music tourism campaign called the

Americana Music Triangle, a list of driving trails and markers in communities around the south to attract tourists to stop and see places they would otherwise drive past.

Nashville, where Aubrey lived, didn't need a strategy, but Aubrey thought that Huntsville, just over an hour's drive away, would be receptive. And to facilitate that discussion, Drew and Aubrey suggested that we do what we did in Brighton — host a conference — this time about music tourism specifically, and invite Huntsville to attend. Like the Great Escape, we partnered with a local music festival, this time the outdoor Pilgrimage Music Festival in Franklin, Tennessee, a town south of Nashville, launching a Music Tourism Convention in September 2017. And as London did in 2015, Huntsville attended. This time we didn't have to stop the event to facilitate a film screening. Working with the local tourism board, Visit Williamson County, we staged the event in a conference hall, across the street from the festival site. 200 professionals attended.

Similar to the Music Cities Convention, we relied on friends and partners as speakers, mainly drawing from Drew and Aubrey's network. We showcased Aubrey's Americana Music Triangle, with many of the destinations already congregating at Pilgrimage's Americana Music Triangle Experience, a tent in the festival where each destination could present themselves to festival attendees. We could utilise our international network and welcome speakers from Canada, the UK and Colombia. And we could drum up business.

It worked. Music tourism, as a standalone sector, had never been defined, much like Music Cities a few years previous, so staging a conference about it was novel. Music attracts people through festivals and events, but music tourism, as a standalone discipline, was limited to cities that proclaimed themselves music destinations, such as Nashville, Austin, Memphis, New Orleans, and cruises offering a tour of America's Music Cities. Yet music is a reason we visit a place as well as something that happens to be there when we're visiting for other reasons. Some diehards, like me, make pilgrimages to specific sites, like the myriad Blues Markers dotted around Mississippi or Graceland. Others experience music passively, such as stumbling upon a piano player at brunch or a passing moment shared with a street performer. Understanding how to strategise both situations was the purpose of the conference.

The widely-held belief was that music was there, and when it was the reason people visited, it was because of an ephemeral shared experience, like a festival. There was little thought that places would benefit from a year-round strategy for music. This was the case before we gathered a few hundred professionals to talk about it.

All places have music. All places can be music destinations, even if they don't have Graceland, Bourbon Street or Beethoven's birthplace. This message penetrated one of the conference-goers — a music representative for a large mixed-use property developer in Huntsville.

We Stopped Going to the Mall

Huntsville, like many low-rise, sprawling American cities, has shopping malls dotted around it. One of those was the Madison Square Mall, set across five city blocks several miles northwest of downtown. Built in 1984 and at nearly one million square feet, it was as unremarkable as any suburban shopping mall in any suburban neighbourhood. It contained what we all wanted at the time under one roof: a food court, clothing stores, movie theatres and concourses for hanging out. By 2016, the mall was in perpetual decline and a property developer from Birmingham, Alabama — RCP Companies — bought it and the land it sat on. RCP had no intention of refurbishing the mall. Instead, it was envisaged as a new mixed-use district, complete with homes and apartments, shops and a new school to service the growing adjacent Research Park neighbourhood, which was overflowing with workers from Redstone Arsenal and its nearby industrial subdivisions.

In the space of a few months, the mall was torn down and this new vision for the area was presented — a mixed-use walkable place to live, close to Redstone Arsenal. RCP Companies CEO Max Grelier and Aubrey had an existing relationship, unbeknownst to me, and when Aubrey caught wind of the plans, which also included an open-air amphitheatre, he suggested that the developer drive the hour north to Franklin and attend the convention. This is how I was introduced to Huntsville.

Huntsville was not incorporated in the Americana Music Triangle. Tourists from Nashville usually drove straight to Muscle Shoals, 70 miles west. Max thought including Huntsville would provide a unique angle to this development, especially as he had planned a new venue in it. Also, like any mid-sized city, Huntsville had a thriving music scene. It just wasn't well known. RCP thought that the Rocket City could be complemented by also becoming a Music City. His new development, called MidCity Huntsville, could be the catalyst to begin this discussion and, if successful, it would be primed to benefit from music being included more in the city's strategic thinking. Investment was needed for the amphitheatre and the RCP needed additional partners to finance, design and operate such a facility. Being a Music City in this case was to better incorporate what Huntsville already had into a vision — mainly of a high-tech, high-wage city — and improve its quality of life indicators, by beefing up music, culture and entertainment.

As I was stage-managing the Music Tourism Convention, I didn't know any of these plans. I had no idea what MidCity was, where it was or its significance. Aubrey had convinced RCP to come and they sent a musician, their arts and culture representative at the time, Shawn Patrick, who had experience as a recording artist in Muscle Shoals. Shawn introduced himself and invited me to Huntsville, which was the first time I had heard of the city. He explained the history of Wernher von Braun; the adjacency to FAME and Muscle Shoals Sound Studios, which was built a little later in 1969 in Sheffield; and the aspirations of MidCity, which included a grassroots music venue and the aforementioned amphitheatre. Shawn read a report Sound Diplomacy issued earlier that year called *The Music Cities Manual* — essentially our first attempt at writing An Idiot's Guide to music ecosystem development. In it was a ten-point plan linking planning, education, tourism, equity, workforce development and other city policies to music, introducing the potential role it could have if it was incorporated intentionally into these areas of policy. Looking back, it was not a detailed nor robust document, but it offered examples and case studies of what we knew after two years of this work. What I didn't know is that RCP had already introduced Sound Diplomacy to the City of Huntsville. RCP had been working on music for months.

The convention was a success, formally introducing the concept of music tourism as a standalone tourism sub-sector. A network was developed to expand the topic and relationships struck to partner to develop it. At the same time, my work with the Mayor of London was slowly coming to an end. I was away from London for nearly a third of the year and, at the same time, the city was immersed in a flurry of activity, including the initial work program from the Night Czar, the continuation of the Night Time Commission and more challenges pertaining to grassroots music venue closures. Improvements were being made and I wasn't there for them. MPs were using pro-music ecosystem talking points in Parliament. The Music Venue Trust's definition of a "grassroots music venue" was widely understood. The London Music Board was meeting regularly. A music tourism campaign, Sounds Like London, was initiated. It was time to take a step away from London and take a step towards the United States and Huntsville.

Max and Shawn believed that if a music strategy was to succeed in Huntsville, the city had to pay, so the work was bipartisan and not commissioned by a private firm with a vested interest. There were other developers in Huntsville also engaging in music and culture, and while they wanted to demonstrate leadership, this was not an area one landowner could control.

After the Music Tourism Convention concluded, I rented a car and drove to Huntsville to meet with Mayor Battle and his team. This began what has been my longest working relationship with a city in America and, in real time, a living lab to better understand how to create and manage a music ecosystem policy from scratch, for better and worse.

Rocket Launch

Other than my work with the Mayor of London and swapping handshakes in crowded receptions surrounded by their advisors, I had never pitched to a Mayor. When I was asked to present to Mayor Sadiq Khan (which happened once and was part of a bigger pitch that was more important than my few minutes), the briefing document had been through dozens of revisions, including being approved by the now Deputy Mayor of Culture, Justine Simons, and her senior advisor Laia Gasch. I was protected from spontaneity because I was a worker bee, far removed from the queen. In civic government, the time senior officials have to make decisions is limited. To get one's point across, one must present a decision in such a way that it can be grasped from all angles in a few minutes, so those in charge can at least defend the decisions they make. Or so it should go. In my time consulting with the Mayor of London, these briefings, press documents and reports went through weeks if not months of edits, at times to ensure that those at the top, with the least amount of time to ponder, had as much information as possible — in that moment — to make a decision. Here, in Huntsville, I was not afforded that luxury. I was by myself pitching an idea full of ambiguity. But I was recommended by one of the city's largest investors.

As I walked towards City Hall, I rehearsed the same points, over and over, in my head:

Music is workforce development.
A song can be a pension.
How music has grown at twice the rate of the national economy over the past decade.
A music venue sustains over twenty types of jobs, from security to bartender, artist to management.
Music increases tourism.
Huntsville can be a world-leading music city.
Don't mention politics of any kind. You don't know what they believe in.
Mention the Space Center. Mention the Rocket City Trash Pandas.

The Trash Pandas are the city's minor league baseball team, an affiliate of the Los Angeles Angels that were moving from Mobile, Alabama, in 2020. And yes, that is their name. I knew the town was excited to welcome them. A new baseball stadium was being built as well, known as Toyota Field, in neighbouring Madison. I felt confident I could create commonality by mentioning the Trash Pandas.

Presenting in these situations is as much an art as a science. I do not believe that it is possible to know the outcome of such a pitch until after it is completed and those on the other side have time to discuss. But I did know that these pitches were a daily occurrence. This is part of their job. The only difference is that this is about growing their music ecosystem. It is still about workforce development, creating a more equitable city, creating jobs and boosting tourism. Just through music this time. And it was a fruitful meeting.

Take Off

Mayor Tommy Battle, his Head of Economic Development, Shane Davis, and Director of Long Range Planning, Dennis Madsen, were kind, courteous and open-minded. True Southern gentlemen from the first handshake. But they had questions.

With little knowledge of Sound Diplomacy and our work in the UK, they had every right to be cautious. We had never completed or implemented a music strategy in the United States. There was no defined proof of concept outside of Austin and Nashville, and both had decades of strategy and investment. Neither of them were known for the space programme, robotics and engineering either. So that is what I did at first, anecdotally pointing to Austin, one of the fastest-growing cities in the United States, and its intentional relationship with music. RCP argued that music could bring more jobs, skills and tourists if a formal strategy was adopted. The key was to look at the wider impact that music could bring on being able to sell the city to investors, or create a more vibrant quality of life to attract workers away from Silicon Valley or Atlanta, and to take a chance on a much smaller, lesser-known city. At the same time, Nashville's geographic proximity presented another reason for them to say no. Why should they care about music when the trademarked *Music City* is 80 miles up the road? Nashville is not the *Rocket City,* so it would make more sense to stick to the existing economic development strategy. But the questions were inquisitive and, instead of the meeting resembling an interview, it was more of a discussion. The discussion topics included:

What would a music audit bring to Huntsville?
How would it improve the city's economic policies and how can we track success?
How can music be a catalyst to support other art forms?
How to do this equitably?
How can we use this to get that amphitheatre built at MidCity?

Their questions were prescient, sharp and inquisitive. A pre-planned 30-minute meeting lasted an hour. But as I had learned later, the sales pitch happened before I entered the meeting. The success of our Music Tourism Convention, a desire to join the Americana Music Triangle and the local endorsements was enough. This was about the detail, the process, the minutiae. The contracting process was initiated a few weeks later.

Huntsville is the fastest growing city in Alabama and was projected to outgrow Birmingham by 2020, becoming Alabama's largest city (and it did just that in 2021).[1] For the city to attract the best companies and with it, a workforce, it must also consider how it packages and sells its quality-of-life offer to prospective investors. This is what underpinned the demolition of Madison Square Mall and its redevelopment into MidCity, a capital investment-led refurbishment of the Von Braun Center and a flurry of redevelopment projects happening around the city, including another $100m-plus development next to the Von Braun Center downtown. At the same time I visited

Mayor Battle, the city was in the throes of its largest ever corporate negotiation outside of Redstone Arsenal, a $2.3bn investment from Toyota and Mazda to construct a car plant outside of town.[2] In addition to these investments, one large entertainment complex was envisaged in the city's long-term strategy, first appearing on a vision document in 2014 — a prospective mid-sized amphitheatre. Before I showed up, music and culture were already on Mayor Battle, Shane and Dennis's minds, along with the rest of their team. RCP Companies submitted plans to include this venue onsite and the city, who owned the land, was open to investing in its development. The stars had aligned.

A Music Strategy in Huntsville

A music strategy is not an off-the-shelf product. It is a collection of research and evidence about where music is in a community, its economic and social value, the barriers it faces to growth and how, through alignment with other policies, to improve conditions for music makers, businesses and audiences. It often leads to something new that's needed. Maybe it's a new music school, or in Huntsville's case, an amphitheatre. Sometimes it's about overruling a particular regulation that negatively impacts musicians and music businesses, as is the case with inequitable and racist frameworks in Madison, Wisconsin, or fixing a lack of alignment between those promoting downtown districts or a city's tourism portfolio, for example. Or it may be something tangential to music but which music helps uncover, such as a stagnant tourism marketing plan, a need to regenerate a particular area, street or part of town, or other issues involving adjacent artforms like theatre, dance or live performance. Or it could be all of these things.

In Huntsville, we developed a menu of data that we wanted to collect based on what we knew. The data would be used to determine where music was, how each component part fit together, how much the ecosystem was worth, what was wrong (or perceived to be wrong) and, if the work would be done properly, how it could be fixed. I knew the information that needed to be collected, but the amount of data had never been mined or analysed before in this way. This was not something we sugar-coated or hid from Huntsville. The existing music ecosystem frameworks, from Music Canada's *The Mastering of a Music City* to our *Music Cities Manual*, were full of overarching frameworks, not quantitative methods. This is what we had to figure out in Huntsville, in real time. And most importantly, do it in public, with the support of as many musicians as possible, as this work was meant to support and help them first. That was the plan.

But I didn't know how these musicians, each unique in their own style, path and objectives, would react to the work. They needed to support it, but it needed explaining, given a music audit was not only new to Huntsville, but to most of the country at that point. These audits, usually called "feasibility studies", were commonplace in other sectors — engineering, planning, construction — but music was new to the process. We were all new to it. Engaging local musicians in the work, and ensuring they saw and recognised that it was being done for them, was objective number one.

If we cared, listened and were honest about the data being collected and the reason for it, we could win people over. Mayor Battle, Shane and Dennis knew that this was not an off-the-shelf product. This was a trial; something new. But one thing I did not realize at the time, but soon became apparent, is that Huntsville was the perfect city for the music audit. Their capital plan and financial security as a city allowed it, as Redstone Arsenal and the thousands of high-skilled jobs it brings with it create property and sales tax revenue. Huntsville's bond rating, their ability to pay back loans essentially, had been rated A+ for over a decade at that point.[3] The city was comfortable with investing in pilot studies and did so all the time, be it supporting start-up engineering companies or manufacturers to relocate there. The format had a framework it could be slotted into, and the argument, that music was nothing special in this regard, just another opportunity to increase Huntsville's quality of life and attract and retain talent, was accepted. The $150,000 contract was signed, plus $15,000 in expenses. This was Sound Diplomacy's largest contract in the United States.

It Didn't Start Well

Every news article chronicling the study led — in its header — with how much Sound Diplomacy was being paid. I wasn't sure if that was the norm in northern Alabama, just part of doing business. I accept the need for transparency, but it stung. It felt like screaming off the page was the subtext: *The taxpayer paid for what? How much? What an outrage.*

That's how I read it and how, I believe, most of Huntsville was first introduced to our work. So from the onset, suspicion set in, with most questioning why this much money was being spent on studying Huntsville's music ecosystem. This was not a project that we could point to and show where it had succeeded elsewhere. We had anecdotal evidence from the Austin and Nashville comparisons — but that was it. In those first few articles written about the study, as well as those published as we worked through the research and presented the findings, the budget allocation was put into a more general context, which assuaged the questioning. In *AL.com* reporter Matt Wake's analysis of our second public meeting, where I presented the survey findings, he made it clear, but this was halfway through the research:

The City of Huntsville is paying Sound Diplomacy $165,000 to conduct the music audit, which began in April. For context, Huntsville corridor studies have cost between $75,000 to $150,000, according to city officials, and the Western Growth Plan, involving Polaris, Toyota/Mazda and GE Aviation development projects, cost $650,000. The Cummings Research Park Master Plan update was around $250,000.

Once the news of the contract went public, we could no longer be shielded by a small group of supporters who understood the need, nature and prospective outcomes of the work. The outcomes that we believed would be delivered by this music ecosystem study, ones meant to impact all levels of city governance, would need to be presented to the public. This was a serious challenge, because the issues the audit aimed to address had never been compared to, or incorporated within, music. The impact on the city's long-term planning, or the potential impact an amphitheatre — if it was agreed to be built — would bring to the city were not, for the most part, concerns of the musicians this work was aimed to directly address. So we organised a public meeting, much like the city does to discuss other civic issues. Billed as a town hall, it was held at a local brewery. The problem was, I was unable to attend. I sent two of our senior staff instead, both experiencing, like I did a few months previous, their first trip to Huntsville and the area.

And the community made it very clear, from the beginning, that we were not going to be welcomed with open arms. We would have to earn their respect and that would involve an intentional, long-term approach, continuing to visit Huntsville to meet with as many locals as possible — one by one — and fulfilling our obligations. I had not anticipated the seriousness and suspicion that the work engendered. It was clear the city was engaged, but they were by no means convinced. And that was going to be made apparent, in person, when we launched the work at the open forum.

But Before That, Over to Muscle Shoals

After meeting Mayor Battle, I drove to Florence, Alabama, an hour's drive to the west. Since the Music Tourism Convention, a similar conversation had been taking place in the Muscle Shoals region. While synonymous with music production because of both FAME and Muscle Shoals Sound Studios, the region, which is made up of four separate communities with different administrations, did not have an intentional approach to music. In an effort to extend the work from Huntsville into Muscle Shoals, time was set aside with the leaders from each community to discuss the idea, and RCP committed to investing in the work. We would produce a separate music audit for the region, but it would be completed at the same time as Huntsville, with the objective of uniting the regions into engaging with music holistically, whilst keeping competition to a minimum.

Muscle Shoals is a music destination, having been home to the recording of some of America's most successful commercial music, from Aretha Franklin's "Respect" to the Rolling Stones' classic "Wild Horses". A 2013 film, *Muscle Shoals*, chronicling the history, renewed interest in the region, and for years pilgrimages were made to tour the studios and take pictures in front of 3614 Jackson Highway, the address of Muscle Shoals Sound Studios in Sheffield, Alabama. But this history was not strategically approached outside of tourism. Each of the four communities — Florence, Tuscumbia, Muscle Shoals and Sheffield — approached music differently. Florence, being the largest of the four communities and home to the local university, was not where either of the famous studios were located. Like Huntsville, or anywhere else for that matter, there was a local scene and talent, but no joined-up approach across city priorities, let alone linking the four communities to approach music collectively across their planning, economic development, tourism, and other policies. But unlike Huntsville, Muscle Shoals was firmly in the Americana Music Triangle, benefitting from the tourism interest it engendered. To entice each community, RCP invested $35,000 in the work. Our ask of each community was $5,000. After my initial visit, a number of additional meetings were organised over the winter and spring to raise the further $20,000 from local officials, including the cities of Florence, Sheffield and the Visit Florence Tourism Board.

In eight months, we had staged a new conference about music tourism and had confirmed over $200,000 in revenue to deliver two music strategies at the same time in northern Alabama. The work, initiated through the support of a few individuals who saw how music could merge self and collective interest, now had a number of cities and public entities invested. There was a lot to prove, given there was no study to point to that demonstrated this works and how the cities would benefit from a music audit. The work began in Huntsville, with a Town Hall meeting at Yellowhammer, a local brewery.

Back to Huntsville

There's footage of the meeting online. It was oversubscribed; standing room only. And it was fractious. We did not plan for this. Town Hall meetings in Huntsville, like any other community, happen every week. Most of the time they are poorly attended as there is limited interest in budget reconciliation, for example. City governments allocate this amount of money all the time on any number of things. Consultants are hired to work on issues no one notices in cities — most cities, in one way or another, have multinational consulting groups such as EY or KPMG on retainer. Roads have to be surveyed; buildings designed, town centres need to be mapped and masterplans need to be drawn. Economic development policies need to be crafted and scrutinised. Consultants are everywhere, including in Huntsville and Muscle Shoals. I should have been there, but I was unable to make it back across the United States. We sent our more senior team members — the ones who will be doing the work. Aubrey Preston, one of the initial connectors whose network led to the work, was also there. As were Shawn, Max and others from RCP, as well as Mayor Battle, Shane and Dennis. Plus, it was a public meeting to introduce something inherently good, however vague at the time. But blindly, assumptively, stupidly, I assumed there was no difference between what we were doing and the work of a traffic surveyor or a town planning consultancy. It was just music.

Music — its messiness, its conviviality, its personal nature, its carnality, its brutality, its lack of order, the fact that it's mine first before it's ours — I underestimated that. I assumed our team would be welcomed as researchers and ethnographers, and this work would be viewed as a research project — unbiased, patient, determined, but of all things, unemotional. Like a master's thesis. This wasn't about any particular type or genre of music. And the audit, as I had envisaged it, was a research project that would come to conclusions after the bulk of the work was done. The community, or some members of it who came to meet us at Yellowhammer, saw it differently. My ignorance, which I feel was adopted by my staff, fuelled this misunderstanding.

Taking time out of their day, for no financial incentive, over 600 local residents and taxpayers, our bosses that we were delivering the music audit for, came to hear two consultants from Europe and a friend of theirs from Nashville discuss the music strategy that they, the taxpayers of Huntsville, had just forked out $150,000, plus expenses, to commission. Many in attendance were struggling to earn $200 a month performing live.

This botched introduction was a symptom of the way that music had been treated in Huntsville, or anywhere for that matter, until the meeting began. Music was not intentionally incorporated into civic discussions, budgets and frameworks. It was not given its own singular set of policies, instead relying on a patchwork of others across planning, alcohol and liquor licensing, event permitting, education and tourism, and as a result, every audience member interpreted music differently, because Huntsville, like most communities at the time, lacked a blueprint to guide them. The way the city spent money to improve quality of life, for example, or public services, had not been independently, singularly, about music. Not only was the concept of a music audit confusing, but the outcomes it would deliver were even more vague, because there was no structure to incorporate them into how the city was being run at that moment. The small number of supporters who helped initiate the work, who came to the Music Tourism Convention or had personal interest in the success of the audit, saw otherwise. The city had a foundation to fit the work into — how it governed economic development. But for the attendees at the meeting, there was no legend, no guide. So success, whatever that meant to each attendee, was unique to them.

Many, buoyed by some free craft beer, welcomed the work and were willing to give it the benefit of the doubt. There was encouragement and to some a relief that the city was investing in music and culture. Others, who took to the microphone most at the meeting, wanted immediate answers to questions we were incapable of answering:

Why were venues requiring artists to play for free?
Why was it so difficult to find a booking agent, or a manager, or a publicist?
Why won't that festival book me?
Why didn't I get to choose who would be involved in this work?
What gives you the right to be an expert in Huntsville's music scene?

None of these questions can be answered by a music audit, but these were the questions many at Yellowhammer that night wanted an answer to. We all frame systemic challenges through our own personal lens. If it happened to me, then it is a collective problem that needs to be addressed. Music, being a personal pursuit, is full of these grievances, due to the competitive nature and often cutthroat reality of the commercial music industry. Few succeed, most fail, but everyone believes they, and their music, deserve a chance. I have come across many artists who are so steadfastly confident in their abilities that there is little leeway for critical thinking. If I believe in my art, my craft, and others don't, then it is their problem, because *I believe in what I am doing.* Moreover, the structural inequalities inherent in all cities, be it access to resources, systemic racism, quality of education offered and who can access it, environmental racism and access to affordable housing, spills over into all local issues, including the state of the local music scene. There is no level playing field in Huntsville. There is no level playing field anywhere. All music scenes have winners and losers, professionals and amateurs, those who access opportunities and those who either lack the opportunity or fail to capitalise on it when it is presented. Some artists simply are not good enough, but some lack access to a field in the first place. Some in Huntsville were earning a living from their music. Most weren't. And everyone wanted to. Everyone in that room felt like that's what their music deserved. I felt this way when I was in a band. I wanted to be heard. I wanted to pursue music professionally. That was all that mattered at the time.

The meeting, albeit at times painful, confrontational and animated, proved, over time, to be one the most successful evenings we had in Huntsville. Hearing, listening and simply being there built trust. We didn't go away.

Music is a profession that few are encouraged by their parents, guardians and educators to take up. It can be ruthless. Few parents dream of their children becoming musicians and many, especially in places where music is seen more as a hobby and less a vocation, are actively discouraged to do so. Music is what you do after work. It's important to learn how to play the piano or the violin, and as such develop a relationship with sound, space and pitch — but thinking that it is a path to paying off a mortgage is another thing altogether. This is a deep-seated prejudice that flows through all of us. We all love music, but it is not a *serious job*, right? And here we are, explaining to musicians, many of whom are not taken as seriously as they should be, that the City of Huntsville is taking music *seriously*. Taking them seriously. And Sound Diplomacy is being paid to listen, collect data about their hopes, dreams, careers, challenges and realities, and report back. This message got across. This was the chance to be taken seriously. But this compounded the challenge we faced. The work was not about any one particular musician, but music as an ecosystem, where if all component parts worked better together, all would benefit.

After two hours of questions, some of the attendees were satiated, others increasingly frustrated and others ambivalent, preferring to wait for the results to make their minds up. But what remained true was, judging by the amount of people that showed up, it was a success. While the event proved stressful, what was lost on the day to us meant the world to Mayor Battle, Shane Davis, Dennis Madsen and the Huntsville City Council. It was one of the best-attended public meetings ever held in Huntsville. The commitment the community showed to music vastly exceeded other public meetings, and the ability for music to be a convening tool for the Mayor's office was made clear. The interest the city showed in music, compared to other issues, far exceeded expectations. Engaging the community is the job of public servants and often, hearings related to traffic, planning, licensing or other civic minutiae are poorly attended unless there's a controversial topic on the agenda. Here, hundreds of residents showed up to hear what the city was doing. Overnight, the value of music to the City of Huntsville expanded. The music audit became a strategic priority.

There's Precedent for This

Few cities have the general revenue or capital budget to invest in a music audit. A music strategy, for most cities, is not in a city budget. There is no *music strategy* line in the general fund next to street cleaning, hiring parking police, picking up rubbish once a week or heating government buildings. But there is no reason why this couldn't be the case. There's precedent for this. Many cities allocate 1% of hotel tax or their general fund to support public art. This includes urban greening, sculptures, murals and other community engagements, and pays artists to do the work. Parks are funded through general-purpose budgets, because they are designed to be available to all for the benefit of the community. In regards to economic development, cities, regions and states have been investing in film and sports commissions for decades. These are staffed offices to attract filmmakers, production companies, sporting teams and events, all of which create jobs. Without large-scale events, hotel rooms are not booked and restaurants lose revenue, so teams are established, jobs are created and paid for, often from general-purpose funds or a percentage of hotel taxes, to work exclusively to attract film, TV or sports. Music is a part of all of these businesses. Few of us stop to think what a basketball or football game would be like without music, or a film or TV show without a soundtrack or soundscape. Music is there, in the background, often part of the supporting cast.

These initiatives, like film or sports commissions or a public art body, all use existing funds from a local tax base. All are tools that cities and places use to promote themselves, attract talent and, if successful, improve the quality of life of residents. Music, bar a few select cities, is not treated with the same care and due diligence. There are very few music commissions, offices and city staff to attract music-related jobs, events and initiatives. Most are located across Northern Europe and Australia, with very few in the Americas or the Global South. As I've outlined, many cities invest in music, but the majority of these investments are ephemeral or site-specific. One solitary venue is used to attract and retain talent, or a weekend over the summer is what communities focus on. While a festival may last for a week or two, including set-up and take-down, there are musicians and entrepreneurs living in the same place all year round. Events and venues are integral elements to ensuring a city or place has an active, engaged and supported music ecosystem, but initiatives in between walls or restricted to particular times of the year are, in essence, restrictive.

Venues, no matter how impressive they are, cannot welcome or cater for all residents, genres and disciplines. Festivals feature some music and ignore others, depending on their priorities and marketing objectives. And when this is the strategy — with focus on a venue, or a festival, or live music in and of itself — a comprehensive, holistic approach to music and the opportunities that knowledge can engender is what's lost. A Sports Commission doesn't call it quits when it attracts one national championship just as landing one Hollywood blockbuster doesn't call an end to a Film Commission's work. It is the opposite. It bolsters it and encourages those working there — who are employed full-time to promote film or sports year-round — to attract more business.

Music is not seen this way because it hasn't been presented in the same way: that a music commission, if funded and invested in, could reap the same rewards as film, sports or public art. Instead, if we have one successful festival, even if it is a month long, that is good enough for the year. Or if there is one successful flagship venue, then little else needs consideration. Millions were spent on the venue anyways.

This is how music is treated: not as a leading actor, but as an ever-present, easy-to-take-for-granted member of the supporting cast. It's there. It'll show up. It can be used, at a minimal cost to support a film, or a sporting event. And we have those festivals as well over the summer, and that terrific concert hall downtown. No need to worry about anything else.

This is changing. There are a number of music commissions in the United States and Europe, from Seattle to Austin, Aarhus to Hamburg. Australia has music offices in each province and a national live music office, the only one of its kind in the world. Many Australian cities, including Melbourne and Perth, are actively engaged in their provincial music office. Every province in France has a music development office and the country as a whole launched the Centre for National Music, or CNM, in 2020 with a budget of €194m.[4] While many of these offices were dedicated exclusively to developing and sustaining local music industries, rather than having a wider perspective on the entire music ecosystem as it links to other city policies, there were models to benchmark and learn from.

Huntsville has a sports commission and a film representative through the Alabama Film Office and the Convention and Visitors Bureau. It also has a public art plan. Huntsville did not have a music commission. So the work began to prove, without a shadow of a doubt, that one was needed.

And So the Work Began

What would a music commission's role be?
Will the music commission lobby to reallocate funds dedicated to other sectors?
Why music? Why not dance or theatre, or looking at the wider creative economy?
How would artists benefit, first and foremost?
What is this strategy going to do for me?
Will it ensure I have better paid gigs?
Will it promote my music?

I didn't have answers to these questions.

But one thing we did have was interest. The city and its musicians and music businesses were engaged, enthralled, curious, questioning and, most importantly, present. I needed an audience for this experiment to work, and the audience showed up.

After the initial Town Hall meeting, the process of completing the music ecosystem audit began. Once all the deadlines and deliverables were agreed, we produced an inception document, which we then published on the city's and Sound Diplomacy's websites, explaining what the work entailed, our contact information, deadlines we would hold ourselves accountable for and the steps that we needed to complete to get paid. RCP Companies provided support on the ground, with Shawn Patrick and another RCP staffer, Nadia Niakossary, assembling stakeholder engagement lists and fielding questions from the public. Once back home in Europe, the desk research, stakeholder preparation and literature review of local regulations, ordinances and bylaws began. For the work to determine what changes should be proposed, we needed to defend them with precedent from other places, as well as develop a deep understanding of Huntsville's bylaws, city codes and wider economic and urban planning strategies. This took a few months and resulted in an assessment of regulations and policies, as well as a comparative analysis against a number of other places. The purpose was to outline what policies impacted the music ecosystem and determine, with evidence, how they were supportive or restrictive to music. Then we outlined who does it better elsewhere and what Huntsville, as a community, can learn from them.

At the same time, we prepared a public survey and confirmed local stakeholders — musicians, music businesses and producers — to participate in roundtables of up to ten people for an hour and a half, which we returned to Huntsville a few months later to conduct. These meetings were supported by an open survey, with separate questions crafted to apply to musicians, businesses and the general public. The questions were both qualitative and quantitative, requesting economic data, the respondent's interest in music, the amount of events people attended and how much they paid for them, as well as general characteristics of the wider music ecosystem in the city.

Artists were asked to provide aggregated income levels to add additional data to the economic impact evidence. Alongside this, the economists assigned to the audit began compiling and coordinating data, which included scraping national and state data sets, along with assessing the survey data and working with local firms to capture their data. The data captured was only partly specific to music.

One challenge in assessing the economic value of music at a local level, and doing it so it encompasses the entire music ecosystem, is the availability of statistical data. The North American Industry Classification System (NAICS), used by both the United States and Canada, is inherently flawed. Each job is given a statistic code, but some jobs in the music industry do not have a code assigned to them. The codes are updated every five years, and we were using the 2017 coding system, which was when it was last updated. Roles pertaining to music streaming, for example, are vague. The code for music streaming services is 518210, which is defined as "Data Processing, Hosting, and Related Services". There are multiple roles, for example, to monetize music streaming — across library music, promotion and aggregation. The complexity of music, and the multitude of types of jobs available in it, are not represented in the classification system. Therefore, the only way to capture reliable local data about a music ecosystem in full is through local engagement. Talking to people. This is what took place in Huntsville.

Over ten months, my team and I made three further trips to Huntsville. Over 1,000 people filled out the survey and several hundred participated in the roundtables. Hundreds of hours of work was put in to review policies and codes and produce a robust assessment that outlined what could be reformed and how to best go about it. In total, seven different researchers and staffers worked on the audit, with the help of a few more locals from RCP.

In October, I returned to Huntsville for a second public meeting to present the survey findings, about two-thirds of the way through the entire process of the audit, joined by Mayor Battle and Shane Davis. In his article titled "Initial Findings of Huntsville's $165,000 Music Audit Are In", covering the meeting, *AL.com* reporter Matt Wake wrote:

> The red-sneakers-wearing CEO contracted to examine Huntsville's music culture and help elevate that culture, thinks "music can tell Huntsville's story as well as space, as well as rockets." Shain Shapiro made that optimistic assertion Wednesday at a public forum to discuss his London-based firm Sound Diplomacy's audit findings thus far. These findings were primarily results from a recently concluded online survey regarding Huntsville local music. The survey received 1,030 completed responses, which Shapiro described as "amazing" feedback for Huntsville's market size. According to 2016 census data, Huntsville's population is 193,079... He also presented survey data he described as "the things we have to work on." This included "the top-five lowest-scoring aspects of Huntsville's music ecosystem in the eyes of music fans," which were, from lowest up, "public transport infrastructure around music venues and festivals"; "variety of music events"; "the reputation of Huntsville as a music city" and "diversity of the local music scene."[5]

I promised the packed auditorium that the final strategy would be submitted to the city by the end of February 2019, four months later. Many in the audience were repeat attendees from the Town Hall launch, but the mood had changed. They were supportive and inquisitive, with many having participated in roundtables or interviews. The meeting was convivial and welcoming. Music continued to bring the community together.

After the public meeting, more work was required. We mapped the music ecosystem in Huntsville, identifying, with the help of RCP and many others, every music-related business and initiative in the city limits, which was plotted on a map and published on the city's website.[6] Once that was completed, all the data that was captured from the regulatory work, stakeholder engagement, surveys and economic analysis was combined to produce a series of recommendations, which were then stress-tested by the city to agree on how it would be implemented, how long it would take and how much it would cost. This extended the work of the audit and I missed the February deadline. Although much of the work was done by then, the process of writing, editing and agreeing on the final report and all it contained, given it would be made public in full, took an additional few months. Once all parties agreed to the recommendations, the various elements were combined into a final strategy and executive summary, which then went through a final editing process with Dennis, Shane and Mayor Battle, as well as select stakeholders.

I arrived back in Huntsville on 16 August, and as per the commitment to the community, delivered a public presentation at the Von Braun Center of the work and what we planned on doing with it. Over 300 people attended the presentation, which I gave with Dennis Madsen, the city's lead on the work. By then, I knew a number of audience members and the mood was ebullient. We had accumulated an extensive amount of data explaining, reviewing and diving deep into Huntsville's music ecosystem, and importantly, how it interacted with — for better and worse — the city's policies. The final report stretched to over 200 pages, and alongside it, we published a 20-page executive summary, knowing full well most would not have the time to read the study in full.

The study contained 47 recommendations, all of which were agreed between February and August. Three days later, I stood in front of the City Council, presenting the findings once more. After a few questions from the five-member board, the strategy was approved, with Dennis being assigned the task of leading its implementation.

Over the course of 16 months, from April 2018 to August 2019, we completed our first music audit in the United States — by far and wide the most extensive piece of work exploring the ins and outs of a city's music ecosystem. In the end, we ended up with a blueprint to replicate in other places, and a humbling feeling that Huntsville, despite the initial reticence, welcomed the work. A few months later, I returned to Huntsville, where Dennis and I, over lunch, reviewed over 100 applications for the city's first music board, which was launched on 23 January 2020 by Mayor Battle. We were retained as consultants to support the board and implement the recommendations, including some changes to the city's bylaws related to event permitting, zoning and artist support. In March 2020, just as the COVID-related lockdowns swept through the United States, the Huntsville Music Board met, a little more than two years to the date I first drove into the city.

Muscle Shoals at the Same Time

The work and process completed in Huntsville was being replicated, at the same time, in Muscle Shoals. Once we finished roundtable discussions in Huntsville, we drove to the Shoals and held roundtables for the music community there. There was less to do, given the smaller population, but the public outreach was just as animated. A public meeting was held at the art deco Shoals Theater in downtown Florence, where a hundred musicians and interested residents peppered me with similar questions to those we fielded in Huntsville. We mapped music assets from each of the four communities — Tuscumbia, Sheffield, Florence and Muscle Shoals — and working with the Muscle Shoals Music Association, Muscle Shoals Sound Studios, RCP and Visit Florence's Canadian-born CEO Rob Carnegie, completed a regulatory assessment, comparative analysis and economic impact. But in Muscle Shoals, the work was focused more on music tourism, as it forms the economic lifeblood of the region, as music is one of the main reasons people travel to the region in the first place. A few years earlier, the film *Muscle Shoals* was released, prompting an upswing in music tourists flocking to Muscle Shoals Sound and FAME Studios to see for themselves where the scores of artists recorded in the 1960s and 1970s, creating some of the most memorable American music of the twentieth century. The legendary house band of the time, the Swampers, remained a core stakeholder in the development of Muscle Shoals' music tourism, as bass player David Hood's wife, Judy, served as the Chairman of Muscle Shoals Sound. David's son, Patterson, co-founded and played in the southern rock band Drive-By Truckers. Talent runs deep here, and unlike Huntsville, Muscle Shoals retained a globally known reputation for being a music destination. So the act of writing a strategy there was confusing to some. The region was a leader in music tourism, but it struggled to retain musicians and entrepreneurs. This work, centred on growing tourism but also geared towards local industrial development — keeping more people here to start businesses, produce albums and write music — was the priority.

That the Muscle Shoals region was perceived by some as hallowed ground created additional challenges to ensure it was comprehensively mapped, assessed and respected. This is another challenge that some communities face. When there is a storied musical heritage or history, it is seen as a success in and of itself. Often, the challenges inherent in other aspects of the place's music ecosystem, such as training and retaining artists or fostering entrepreneurs, are ignored. This is not what was intentionally happening in Muscle Shoals, but when something is popular, it is prioritised. Tourism was the game.

Like Huntsville, the Shoals region had a number of living and thriving music assets, businesses and entrepreneurs. Single Lock Records, owned by alternative folk artist John Paul White, was based there. FAME and Muscle Shoals were still working studios, recording modern artists including the Black Keys and Jason Isbell. What was lacking in the region, however, was a joined-up approach, shared by all four municipalities and other third-sector organisations on how to treat music as an ecosystem and move forward with a unified plan, which would make more out of the rich tourism assets while not solely relying on the past. The four municipalities were not aligned in recognising and governing their music ecosystems. For example, zoning bylaws — how loud, where and for how long music could be aired in public spaces — were different depending on whether one was in Florence or Tuscumbia. Building codes were not structured to recognise and understand the impact of a music venue and a hotel or block of flats being side-by-side. This disjointed approach was evident, and it cost them.

In the summer of 2018, a new hotel opened on Florence's main street, North Court St.[7] This investment was welcome news for Florence, a town with a bustling main street economy but lacking in downtown accommodation. Housed in the former Belk Hudson Department Store, the Stricklin' Hotel opened in time for the famous W.C. Handy Blues Festival, which encircles downtown Florence every July, bringing thousands of tourists to the region. However, it shared a wall with FloBama, a music venue and restaurant that had been in business in downtown Florence since 2010. Florence did not have an Agent of Change provision enshrined in municipal code, so adequate sound mitigation would have been required so both businesses could coexist. One month after opening, the new hotel sued the existing music venue, due to noise. Guests were unable to sleep.

This story is not unique. As we have already seen, this is an underlying reason for a number of music venue closures in London, where new residential accommodation, be it homes or hotels, was built next to existing venues with little regard for their existence. People move in, complain, litigation begins and the venue closes. And everyone loses money. It is standard practice in cities that do not enact policies to support their music ecosystems. The music venue, FloBama, was in business first, and if the rules were in place to respect both businesses, the hotel would have been required to recognise that live music took place next door. This was an example of a business ecosystem that took music for granted, without recognising its needs. Both parties understood the risk, as local television station WAFF reported:

> Now here's what's important. FloBama is a restaurant and music venue that has been open since 2010. Hotel developers knew that going into the project. Developers strategically placed guest rooms on the other side of the hotel away from the music venue in hopes of avoiding noise from FloBama.[8]

Recognising a risk and dealing with it when it is realised is different. Many buy homes in flood plains, get flood insurance and are still surprised when their home is flooded. Knowing the venue was there wasn't enough if one is paying for a room and unable to sleep in it. Guests began demanding refunds. The civil case was eventually settled, but it never had to happen in the first place. In a region known globally for its music, the city of Florence lacked the foresight to recognise that installing clear requirements in city code related to new developments near existing noise-making businesses would make sense, especially if a new hotel and a music venue share walls. It was left to chance, instead of there being definitive and intentional guidelines for both parties. This happens over and over again. It sometimes causes consternation and, in some cases, like this one, litigation. If that money would have been spent on developing Florence's music ecosystem, the return would have been much greater.

It was these situations that the work had hoped to address and, like in Huntsville, the community engagement, trust and dedication to the process in Muscle Shoals was heartening after the initial suspicion wore away at the beginning of the work. Also like in Huntsville, I returned to town to present the results in person, this time on 19 October 2019, at the riverside Marriott Hotel, whose bar and lounge is dedicated to Muscle Shoals' music heritage.

It was a stressful day. Inclement weather delayed a flight from Denver to Nashville, and I was 45 minutes late for the presentation. Thankfully, Shawn Patrick from RCP kept the audience entertained and the bar was open, but I arrived flustered and embarrassed. I had never been late for a public presentation before. I received the benefit of the doubt and, after sharing the results, the response was similar to Huntsville's — the same data sets were analysed and presented and those in attendance welcomed the recommendations. A report in the local *Quad Cities Daily* newspaper read:

The study found that music, in its totality, is worth $49m annually to The Shoals' overall economy with The Shoals region outpacing the per capita per-person value of music, which is $678 (compared with $444 nationally). This equates to 479 jobs, or 1.6% of the total workforce and 1% of the total economic output of the area. Already, a number of initiatives have taken place to expand this number, including the development of new venues and the reforming of entertainment and licensing regulations in both Florence and Sheffield. The study makes the case that by further harmonizing cultural district, noise and street performance regulation, The Shoals can further expand its music tourism offer and increase its presence as a recording hub. At the same time, more sustained partnerships have been struck across North Alabama, via an initiative linking FAME Studios with RCP Companies' MidCity development and more partnerships with music associations in the region.[9]

In just 18 months, we had completed comprehensive music strategies in Huntsville and the Muscle Shoals region, and so other cities and organisations began to take interest. Over that year, we signed new contracts, including one with the Walton Family Foundation to deliver a music strategy for the northwest Arkansas region, in Tulsa, Oklahoma, Indianapolis, Indiana, San Francisco and Fort Worth, Texas, who had recently become the first "Music Friendly City" through a new economic development initiative led by the Texas Music Office, which is a department of the Governor's Office. The idea with a Music Friendly City was to provide a template to any community to recognise, map and invest in their music ecosystems. If they did so, including mapping music assets, creating an events calendar or database of musicians and installing a taskforce to represent music in civic discussions, the Governor would declare the community "music friendly".[10] The only such program in the nation, Fort Worth became the first such city in 2018. 40 cities have followed and more are going through the process. Fort Worth's commitment to the designation was to conduct an economic impact study.

Sound Diplomacy, through the trust of Huntsville and Muscle Shoals — and those that introduced us to the region — was thriving in the United States. But none of the work had results to point to yet. These were to come. The first step was to help Huntsville realise the amphitheatre at MidCity.

The Orion Amphitheater

Huntsville is a tertiary market in the commercial music industry. It is equidistant to Nashville and Birmingham, where if there was a show in either city, you could drive there and return in the same evening. It is also close to Atlanta, another major music market. Muscle Shoals is an hour down the road. Artists more than often drove through Huntsville rather than stop to play there. When I first visited Huntsville when the audit began, there was no venue larger specifically dedicated to music than the Mark C. Smith Hall at the Von Braun Center, which had 1,955 seats. The Probst Arena, part of the Von Braun complex could host 9,000, but it was used primarily for sports.

Long before I arrived, there had been discussions at City Hall about building an amphitheatre. The site of the old Madison Square Mall, MidCity, was one option. Another was on a plot of land downtown. In my first visit to RCP's offices, before I met with the Mayor's Office and the Town Hall meeting launched the work, the firm's CEO, Max Grelier, explained the situation. A letter of intent had been signed with a multinational concert promoter and discussions were ongoing about a potential site for a standard amphitheatre with a stage, seating and a lawn that would be expected to host 20 to 25 concerts per year. It was anticipated that the city would pay for the construction of the venue, in exchange for a percentage of revenue on top of taxes and fees. It was part of the city's ten-year strategic plan, along with attracting automotive manufacturers, expanding Redstone Arsenal and building more housing downtown. It was a priority alongside other priorities.

In terms of the commercial music industry, Huntsville sits in the middle of touring routes used by both Live Nation and AEG, the two largest players in the market. Each owns properties that Huntsville concertgoers could drive to, including AEG's Ascend Amphitheater in Nashville and Live Nation's subsidiary Red Mountain Entertainment's Oak Mountain Amphitheater in Pelham, Alabama, outside of Birmingham. Tuscaloosa, home to the University of Alabama and less than an hour's drive from Huntsville, also boasted an amphitheatre, also run by Red Mountain Entertainment. With these venues come radius clauses — artists booked to play were restricted in booking other dates within a certain geographic radius to maximise the available audience who would purchase tickets. Huntsville, being geographically equidistant to both Nashville and Birmingham, as well as Tuscaloosa, Muscle Shoals and even Atlanta, inferred that if it was to build a venue of comparable size, and have its venue run by one of these two multinationals exclusively, the other firm's artists would be heavily restricted to play there. At the same time, most amphitheatres on non-show days are closed. Like American football stadiums or professional soccer stadiums, they are more than often single-use buildings. When there's no gig, there's no footfall.

Being in discussion for several years prior to my visit, realising an amphitheatre in some capacity would be wound into the deliverables of the music audit. I have no experience in designing, managing or booking amphitheatres, but I understood radius clauses and how the live sector operated. What Huntsville needed was a destination amphitheatre, for both consumers and artists, so it didn't matter that all these other major markets were nearby. People would have to want to come to Huntsville to see live music. Artists would have to want to perform there, because what an artist requests is usually what happens. This was the general idea, while pouring over blueprints in RCP's office. So, from the beginning, Huntsville opening an amphitheatre in a few years was a part of the audit process.

After signing the contract, I knew I needed help. I needed to speak to someone who had experience operating large music venues and, if possible, amphitheatres. I believed anecdotally that the best path forward was for the amphitheatre to be managed independently, so it could book any artist, no matter who represented them. If it was run at arm's length from the multinational concert promoters, but in partnership with them, it would be available to more artists, but would still attract the big artists who people wanted to see and pay upwards of $50 or $60 for, without whom the venue would not be viable. Also, I had recently visited Colorado on the trip where I was late for the public presentation in the Shoals, and while there, took a tour of Red Rocks, a 9,500-capacity venue built into a rock face outside Denver. Red Rocks, being in a public park, was open year-round to residents to walk around, exercise in and explore, only closing to the public before soundcheck on show days. It functioned as an exercise facility, picnic area and tourist attraction, as well as a concert venue — I thought, without much evidence, that Huntsville's amphitheatre should be similar. Looking at its location on the periphery of MidCity's new mixed-use district, we thought that, for it to best support as much of the music ecosystem as possible, it should also be open year-round as much as possible, rather than fenced-off when closed, which would be upwards of 250-300 days per year. If this was designed into the development, then it could also function as a community centre or host corporate or neighbourhood events, food fairs, pop-up ice rinks and vintage clothing markets. Also, if the venue was to be built at MidCity as intended, it would be encircled by a public park. Huntsville's relatively clement weather also helped.

The first person I called was an old friend I had met a decade previous, a concert promoter named Mike Luba. Mike was part of the team that developed the Forest Hills Tennis Stadium in Queens into an open-air music venue, and through his firm, Madison House Concerts, was responsible for a number of seminal experiences of my youth, having worked with the Grateful Dead, String Cheese Incident and many other jam bands that share a musical scene with Phish. Luba understood Huntsville, having grown up nearby. He was familiar with the discussions of Huntsville building an amphitheatre, as the live sector in America's southeast is managed, at the top, by a small group of individuals. Over tapas and a beer in midtown Manhattan, Luba listened as I told him we'd been hired to deliver a music strategy and that one of its objectives was to develop an amphitheatre. While busy with Forest Hills, Luba told me that the best person to approach was Ben Lovett, who played in Mumford and Sons and had just recently launched his own live firm, the Venue Group. Luba had promoted Mumford and Sons' Gentlemen of the Road tour, which took the band to small venues and underutilised spaces around America, including a part of the tour where the band travelled by train, performing in small towns along the way. Luba was an experienced promoter, able to make something out of nothing. And he did not need to be convinced about Huntsville. He knew its opportunity, its growth and the catchment area. Thankfully, I had already met Ben a few months before, so he took my call.

I had met Ben at City Hall in London in late 2016, when he was opening a new grassroots music venue in a railway arch in south London called Omeara. This was the same time I was consulting with the Mayor of London's Culture Team, working as the secretariat of the London Music Board. Ben and I became friends. I supported the development of Omeara by introducing Ben and his team to relevant policymakers in London, and Ben, having learned that I was relocating to New York for the summer in 2017, offered me free office space at his Brooklyn-based headquarters during my stay. Spending six weeks with his team at his Fort Greene headquarters cemented this relationship. I agreed with Luba — if Ben was not interested, he would at least know who I could approach.

I had no idea that Ben would be interested in Huntsville. But I knew that, in theory, a partnership between Ben, Mike and other industry heavyweights would offer the approach I pitched to Max, and later the city, of an independently-run, community-focused venue. I asked Ben what he thought. He immediately asked for a meeting with the city.

In August 2018, four months after we had begun the work in Huntsville, our London office and staff moved in with Ben's company at their offices in south London, taking the top floor of the building next to his venue, Omeara. This proximity further accelerated the partnership, giving his team more insight into the audit. Given the amphitheatre was a blank slate, our collective pitch was that, if it was to be successful, it needed to cater to the experience of both the audience and artist. If an artist wants to play a venue, that is often the only justification needed to book it. Having Ben, an artist who had played hundreds of these venues, as part of the design team would ensure that the artist's experience was catered for as much as the audience's. All the minutiae of catering to artists and their crews, including the services available backstage, loading and unloading capabilities, sightlines and other key features were requirements Ben and his team knew. In addition, he understood how to plan a venue where there was no bad seat and every consumer was cared for and catered for. He operated a mini version of this at Omeara. His firm also managed adjacent arches, which featured a food hall with independent producers.

On Ben's request, I introduced him, Luba and their team to Max and the team at the city, including Mayor Battle. He was as amazed by the Rocket City as I was. By January 2019, a design contract had been signed confirming the relationship, and Ben, Mike and their team, along with Max and others, organised a series of design charrettes, including one that I participated in during the Voodoo Festival in New Orleans in October 2019. On 22 January 2020, a year later, the city committed $40m to building the amphitheatre at MidCity. The Huntsville Venue Group was born.

Opening Night at the Orion

Eighteen months before the amphitheatre was to open, the Huntsville Venue Group, now led by Ryan Murphy, the former director of the St. Augustine Amphitheater in north Florida, announced a date. On 7 May 2022, they would hold a soft launch fundraiser for Huntsville Regional Hospitals and the following weekend, 12-14 May, the venue would open. Committing to a particular date that far in advance, during a period where pandemic-related lockdowns and an emerging supply chain crisis restricted access to certain building materials, was full of risk. But despite all this, the venue opened on time, with local artist Jake Owen playing the hospital fundraiser and local artist John Paul White as the first artist to perform on May 12th.

By the time it opened, the amphitheatre had been rebranded as the Orion, to reference and celebrate the local history with space exploration. An opening weekend festival had been booked called The First Waltz, featuring artists with links to Huntsville and north Alabama, including Jason Isbell (from Florence), Emmylou Harris (originally from Birmingham) and Brittany Howard (former frontwoman of Alabama Shakes and from Athens, 30 miles down the road). Features appeared in *Rolling Stone* and the *Wall Street Journal* celebrating its opening, with many articles,[11] including one in Southern culture magazine *Garden and Gun*, featuring interviews with Ben.[12] Matt Wake's detailed review of the opening weekend, the same journalist who dissected each release of the audit, was celebratory.[13] The Orion, quickly after opening, became the anchor of Huntsville's music ecosystem. A calendar of events including scientist Neill Degrasse Tyson, the Black Crowes and Jack White was booked. As was promised, a local food market encircled the amphitheatre. The Huntsville Venue Group leased and began planning an indoor downtown venue called the Lumberyard.[14] On the same night of the opening of the Orion, Brooks and Dunn played a sold-out show at the Von Braun Center.[15]

This success and recognition demonstrates that when a music ecosystem is supported, the most highlighted aspects of it are recognised even more. On its face, the building is an 8,000-capacity outdoor amphitheatre in a mid-sized regional city. But to those who attended, it was much more. As Anna Steele reported in the *Wall Street Journal*:

> Adam Cantrell is used to driving two or three hours to see a concert. The 39-year-old live music fan has lived in Huntsville, Ala., his entire life. He has driven to

Birmingham, Atlanta and Nashville — just far enough to warrant an overnight stay. Now the big-name acts are coming to him. He recently saw Kenny Chesney and Dierks Bentley right in Huntsville at the new Orion Amphitheater, and said he plans to see Chris Stapleton there later this month. He might be able to see six shows there for the price of one show further away, he said.[16]

Plotting the prospective economic impact of the venue as a tool to retain concert-goers who were attending concerts elsewhere was a seminal argument for stumping up the cash to build it. But the process of how this happened, and the challenges along the way, were not wholly understood or evaluated in the public discussions of the venue as it was being developed. The cost-benefit analysis was often discussed in a crude, binary fashion based on the total bill at the end versus how much and when the city would cover its costs and eventually, as was predicted, turn a profit.

The Orion was first budgeted at $40m. This included remediating the land, building a new slip road from the adjacent motorway to support traffic and egress, and the design and build of the venue itself. In the end, it cost close to $48m. Not all local councillors approved of the spend — despite being in line with similar capital infrastructure projects like the minor league baseball stadium, some councillors expressed the opinion that the money could be better spent elsewhere. Ensuring equitable access to the facility, so that it was made as available as possible to as many residents as possible, was also questioned throughout the construction, ideation and planning process. Murphy presented to Huntsville City Council multiple times, including on 21 September 2021, eight months before the opening of the venue, sharing a presentation outlining the free community-based events the venue would commit to staging.[17] Not only was the total cost as a capital infrastructure project questioned, the manner in which the venue was sold as a concept to the community was scrutinised. Some suspicions that influenced the initial meeting at Yellowhammer Brewery when the audit began remained. But after a number of council presentations and press announcements, it was clear that a commitment to the audit enhanced community support and interest as it was being built. Having data and evidence allows a forum for these issues — cost, programming and equity — to be aired and addressed. Murphy continued to update the city council, and as the construction took shape and images were shared of a half-built structure, he and I also participated in meetings with the Huntsville Music Board, ensuring that the community was kept up to date with the construction and how the venue supported the audit findings. This process — overt engagement, publicising more than most and leading with data and evidence — is one that few cities had normalised. And it demonstrated the excitement of these developments in Huntsville. This process required a commitment to invest first $165,000, then over $40m in a music venue. It required a commitment to recognising the value of music to one's talent attraction and retention strategy, alongside tourism and developing the music industry as a standalone goal. And most importantly, it required a commitment to gathering evidence and acting on it, and letting it then drive public policy rather than public policy driving evidence.

As a result, a landmark facility that has responded to and acted on the audit recommendations is staging its second season of concerts. It has welcomed learning tours from other communities, including Macon, Georgia, who are building their own facility, and Monroe, Alabama, who are embarking on the redevelopment of their 1960s civic centre, the Jack Howard. And Ben's firm, rebranded as tvg hospitality, has secured $50m in investment from a host of sources to expand its footprint, with Huntsville as a model.[18] In September 2022, a feature in *Rolling Stone* chronicled this success, with a picture of a packed Orion front and centre.[19]

To ensure further commitment from the city, this is not enough. Policy requires policymakers, and for music, that is often left to individuals with other jobs, as it was in Huntsville with Dennis Madsen, the city's long-range strategic planner. Another recommendation in the audit was to appoint a full-time music officer — a public sector job to represent and engage with the music ecosystem and act as a liaison between the private sector, community and administration. This took longer than expected in Huntsville due to the repurposing of funds to combat pandemic-related needs, but it happened. By the end of 2021, Huntsville had its own music officer.

Huntsville's Music Officer

As we have seen in the examples discussed so far in this book, if something is not recognised in policy, there isn't a process for it to be included in government business. This leads to bad policy-making, like in Melbourne and Sydney, where music policy was being wound into issues of alcohol and liquor licensing. When trouble occurs, someone needs to take responsibility for fixing it.

This is why cities need one person responsible for their music policy. This was the intention with the Music Officer position, one Huntsville not only needed but deserved after investing a large amount of time, money and community spirit in the audit. The job description went through several edits and, in July 2021, the city announced the creation of the position through a press release. And as to be expected, the city received more applications for this position than any other in city history. Here's the city's take:

> The City of Huntsville is now accepting applications for Huntsville Music Officer, a full-time position geared toward anyone with a vision for transforming the Rocket City into a must-see music city. The City is in a prime position to draw regional and national music fans who want to catch a show at the Mark C. Smith Concert Hall at the Von Braun Center or the new Mars Music Hall. At MidCity, construction is underway on an 8,000-seat outdoor amphitheater expected to attract artists from a myriad of genres. "Music is essential to not only our quality of life, but also our local economy," Mayor Battle said. "No matter who you are or what your background is, music is a universal language that unites us all. There's no reason why Huntsville can't be a top destination for musicians and music lovers, and we believe the Music Officer will help us get to that level." City leaders anticipate significant interest in the position but want someone who is not only a creative thinker, but also understands the value of Huntsville's music scene in both cultural and economic terms. "The Music Audit offered a road map, but the Music Officer will need to work very closely with the Music Board to make adjustments and guide implementation," said Dennis Madsen, Huntsville's manager of Urban & Long-Range Planning. "They'll need to develop their own strong relationships with organizations like the Convention and Visitors Bureau and Arts Huntsville, with venues large and small, and especially with artists and industry professionals.[20]

The position, as designed, would oversee strategic planning initiatives and be responsible for implementing the recommendations in the audit. The person in the role would also identify, implement and increase music-related economic opportunities while being a primary point of contact for local, regional and national stakeholders. Candidates would serve as a liaison between both government officials and those in the music industry. "The ideal candidate will have to have a lot of initiative," Madsen said.

Local reporter Matt Wake said this:

> While Huntsville's never produced a mainstream-famous band, there's no shortage of talented musicians from this area, some of whom have toured internationally, produced/ written music for superstar acts and/or been a part of major label bands. Huntsville is also home to a number of successful behind-the-scenes industry professionals, including roadies and guitar techs for famous artists. There are also some rising singer/songwriters, rappers and bands from Huntsville worthy of a shot at the next level. So there's definitely a lot to build with here. And potentially build up. With the 2020 addition of Von Braun Center's gleaming Mars Music Hall, and the Huntsville Amphitheater set to debut in 2022, the city's live venue portfolio is about to become the strongest it's ever been.[21]

More music related changes were happening at the same time. Murals of Little Richard have popped up all over town, celebrating and honouring the legend who is buried in Huntsville.[22] New music education programs have been initiated, including by the Maitland Music School and the University of North Huntsville.[23] The Huntsville Venue Group held a job fair. Music, as an ecosystem, is part of Huntsville, and its new Music Officer, Matt Mandrella, is in place to safeguard and develop it.[24]

Huntsville's music ecosystem is active, engaged and treated seriously by the city and its residents. And it is this seriousness, a way of looking at music in all forms and functions, that demonstrates the value a music ecosystem policy can engender. Music is not special in Huntsville. It is simply given the same level of dedication, seriousness and data gathering as any other sector that a city, and its people, care about.

At the same time, similar initiatives took place in Muscle Shoals. Judy Hood, the Chairman of the Muscle Shoals Music Association, began working with amphitheatre boss Ryan Murphy and the Huntsville Venue Group to create a more sustained bond between the two places. Jason Isbell, Hood and others launched Shoals Fest, a new contemporary music festival that takes place in October.[25] The Muscle Shoals Music Association gained new employees and through them has launched networking events for musicians to encourage them to record in the region — Chris Stapleton and Willie Nelson, for example, have committed to do just that.[26] A new tax incentive for sound recording was launched by the Muscle Shoals Regional Economic Development Association, offering up to 30% reimbursements for projects recorded in the region.[27] Muscle Shoals, like Huntsville, acted on the data and evidence it now had, and with it, a more engaged narrative emerged. Music was not only a part of tourism, but also how to create new jobs.

Far More Work to Do

Huntsville, however, has not avoided the impact of the COVID-19 pandemic. Musicians in Huntsville, as they have everywhere, lost or were denied significant revenue opportunities. Many left the profession. But throughout the pandemic, the Music Board continued to meet. With its Music Officer, Music Board and all local music ecosystem stakeholders, as well as its understanding of their music ecosystem, the city was responsive to the needs of musicians. And importantly, the existence of these frameworks increases resilience. Huntsville is better prepared for future shocks and better poised to capitalise on opportunities, because it knows what it has, how it fits together and how to work as one to further the music ecosystem. It has become a city that invests in, cares for and treats its music ecosystem with respect. This is the process that Huntsville has embarked on and, in 2022, for the first time, they were recognised as the "Best Place to Live" in the United States.[28] This is not only because of music, but the commitment to music and what it can deliver for communities is part of this accolade, and one that is being recognised nationally. This commitment is not led by us, but by hundreds of local musicians and businesspeople, who listened, provided information and participated in the audit, many of whom approached me for an embrace during the opening weekend of the Orion. Both in Huntsville and Muscle Shoals, musicians led the process, and through it further revealed the untapped economic might they hold, and how music, if treated intentionally, can empower a place.

Where it goes now, no one is sure. But the work itself is no longer the blueprint; Huntsville and Muscle Shoals are. They are *the* music ecosystem city and region, places that have taken time and resources to understand the role of music in its community, and are reaping the benefits from it.

Is This the Blueprint?

Can this happen anywhere? I believe it can. In its own way, it happens every day in London, Melbourne, Madison, Berlin and thousands of other cities. It requires a blueprint, influenced by Huntsville and Muscle Shoals, but one that is general enough to provide a framework for any community that wishes to invest in its music ecosystem. Huntsville, like all communities, is unique — buoyed by Redstone Arsenal and the consistent, long-term tax base that it brings, it had the resources to invest in a music audit, whereas other communities may not think that they do. Muscle Shoals has a musical heritage few can match. But there is much that we can learn from both to take forward. This work focused on understanding a community, not dictating to them. It was guided by research, which took time. It never assumed anything. It showed, rather than told, once the data revealed a particular issue or area of concern. And it is not a panacea, but the beginning of a process. It is this process that forms the blueprint, a guide that any city, any community, can pursue should they wish to. It is about recognising that music matters, and that if something matters, it requires time, effort and money.

So in the next chapter, here is the blueprint.

CHAPTER 5
THE BLUEPRINT

First things first — a music ecosystem policy is not only about music. It creates a framework to understand how music impacts other place-based policies, so it must be written as such. The goal is to improve the external impact music has on communities, as well as create a sustainable commercial music industry. Delivering affordable housing, for example, touches on music policy. If environmental health, noise and soundscape requirements are not up to standard, homes built close to existing bars, music venues and nightclubs could provoke noise complaints if they are not built to appropriate standards, for example if they don't have insulation and double-glazed windows, if the balconies are poorly-placed or if the building materials are below-par. Music isn't a primary concern here, but not recognising the impact it can have on new homes is a flaw. Having a policy that outlines the role that music plays — however minimal — in affordable housing delivery, can reduce potential issues in the future.

The Agent of Change principle is a case in point. While on the surface it appears to be a policy to support music venues and nightclubs, it is equally about ensuring that good housing can be delivered anywhere, and that those who want to live in entertainment and cultural districts can do so — and still get a good night's sleep. This is the same for any noise-making industry, such as heavy manufacturing, or other land uses such as agriculture. If someone moves next to a pig farm and complains about the smell, then it is not the farmer's fault. Pigs smell. Music can be loud. Ensuring these standards are adhered to protects the music and those that rely on it for their livelihoods, but more importantly it supports wider civic social cohesion. If developers build appropriately insulated homes in noisier districts, they will be more lucrative and, over time, profitable, given the desire to live in so-called vibrant communities. More land available in town centres — through building outward or upward — creates more space for housing, much of which is sorely needed. There is no reason why homes can't be above music venues, shopping malls and other cultural and entertainment uses, if they have sufficient soundproofing, insulation and are built properly. This requires a policy, so it can be monitored and enforced.

Incorporating a music ecosystem policy into civic governance is a protective measure that helps foster community cohesion and limit conflict. As cities recover from the impact of COVID-19, we are seeing fewer office workers in town centres and downtowns. A subsequent drive to convert more empty buildings into homes will be seen as an opportunity to satisfy two policy objectives at once — more housing and regenerating quiet business districts. When live music returns, it's important that it works in unison, not in competition with these objectives. However, this has not been the case, and many communities that lack a cohesive music policy are seeing an uptick in noise complaints, as people return to bars, restaurants and public spaces.

Noise complaints surged during the first lockdown, mainly due to neighbours playing music too loud.[1] The result is a host of communities rewriting their sound and noise ordinances to restrict decibel levels. Even cities like New Orleans, whose evening and night-time economy thrives on outdoor live music, is rewriting its noise ordinance, where music is equated to intrusive noise, as longstanding music magazine *Offbeat* put it, leading to further restrictions.[2] Without a policy to represent music in all forms and functions, music and noise are seen as the same thing which is why until August 2022, performing outdoor music was illegal in New Orleans.[3]

This is the key component to understanding why creating and maintaining a music policy matters in every community. Much of the work is not about music. It is about recognising — both good and bad — the impact that music has on communities, and thinking intentionally about how to best support, mitigate and understand it. This is about the built environment — everywhere — and all those who share it — everyone.

One trap that places sometimes fall into is prioritising becoming a "Music City" or investing in winning a particular accolade, such as the one given by UNESCO's Creative Cities Network. The badge can be a powerful influence, but once the accolade is won, the work must reflect the requirements to ensure the music ecosystem is being incorporated into wider discussions and policies around the built environment. It should not simply be a marketing tool to promote music.

There are a number of cities that have put in the work to earn the designation as a UNESCO City of Music, but that's it. A few of the links on UNESCO's website cataloguing these cities direct to non-existent websites, or contacts whose emails bounce back. These types of badging — such as European or UK Cities of Culture; or Years of Music that many cities, such as St. Paul, Minnesota, Chicago and others — have staged, often prioritise celebration over long-term investment. For example, Congo-Brazzaville, a city full of musicians and talent, is in a country that lacks legislation to protect intellectual property. If a local Congolese artist wished to pursue a music career, they would be best suited to move or register their works with a foreign collective management organisation, despite the will, drive, expertise and commitment of local stakeholders to develop the city's music ecosystem. Without a national framework to support music, it is nothing more than a badge. Moreover, there is a tendency to singularly place budgets within a Cultural Office, and in doing so the needed links across departments and policy areas, from workforce development to tourism, are not as strong as they could be.

Music and culture tend to have to advocate for relevance internally, rather than being part of a holistic, cohesive framework that places music into all city policies. Being a "City of Music" does not mean that the planning system will better incorporate the needs of music, or more robust intellectual property regulation will be lobbied for in places that lack it. It means that a city brands itself as one that celebrates music. It does not mean that the city and its music ecosystem are any better off because of it.

This type of front-facing marketing, which can celebrate an entire city, a community or a particular artist, is a single objective. There is no understanding of music's interlocking relationship with wider built-environment policy. Instead, it is one department — culture or tourism, usually — focused on one solution, for one aim. And within each of these solutions, other elements of the music ecosystem are forgotten. The challenges facing Congo-Brazzaville's musicians remain, including access to the global market, support from effective and transparent copyright and access to music education, along with human rights issues like literacy, housing, access to clean water and workers' rights. These issues are not specific to music, but they underscore the challenge here and the mindset shift needed to overcome it. When music is siloed, its impact is siloed.

There are many policy questions that form each element of the music policy blueprint. If a city creates a Music Board,

Music Commission or Music Office, then what objectives does it want to achieve within the city's wider strategic framework that isn't directly musical? Is the Music Board codified into city policy, or is it a voluntary initiative with little regulatory bite or influence? If the city is committed to carbon neutrality by 2030 or 2050, is there a set of goals that the Music Office proposes so its objectives and deliverables can be included in the targets? And is it monitored and assessed (which costs money)? How can a Music Office, Board or Commission support affordable housing policy to not only ensure artists are included, but that the housing is also built in such a way that we can enjoy a night out or a good night's sleep, no matter where we lay our heads? Does the Music Office understand and influence local tax policy, and has evidence been put forth to ensure that music-making, music businesses and music venues are able to apply for incentives? Is music and culture a key sector for the Chamber of Commerce or Economic Development Council? Is there a direct relationship between music-makers and destination marketers, so the most varied music offer available can be included in how the city is promoted? What about education policy? Are there frameworks in place to ensure music education is accessible to everyone, regardless of their income level?

A robust music policy provides answers to these questions.

A Robust Policy Blueprint

If we separate music into the same designations that govern other built-environment policies, a policy blueprint emerges that can be adapted to local needs, whatever they may be. The requirements of a music policy in Congo-Brazzaville are different to those in Huntsville, Alabama.

But these cities share the fact that each place is home to musicians, music listeners and policymakers. Each has homes, bars, restaurants and schools. Each is impacted by our changing climate and needs to be more resilient. Each is planning for its future, taking decisions now to improve lives later. And each governs under similar overarching frameworks — economic development and job creation, social issues, education, development and regeneration, tourism, and health and safety. Music factors into all of these, and better understanding the entry and exit points will help define — and refine — one's music ecosystem policy. Here are the key policy areas to take forward that form the blueprint.

Music and Economic Development

The World Intellectual Property Organization (WIPO) stated in a 2015 article that

> a vibrant music economy drives value for cities in several important ways. It fuels job creation, economic growth, tourism development and artistic growth, and strengthens a city's brand. A strong music community also attracts highly skilled young workers in all sectors for whom quality of life is a priority. This, in turn, attracts business investment.[4]

The minutiae of what makes up a vibrant music economy is based on the success of a local constituency's industrial or commercial music economy. If musicians are supporting themselves and their families, venues are filled and festivals well attended, these assets can be tools to attract business investment. Likewise, a famous festival, venue or artist drives interest. But the outcomes are reliant on a number of economic development policies — across geographic, political and jurisdictional boundaries — that often have nothing to do with music but still impact the role it plays.

If music is to be seen as a sector that can drive economic development and inward investment, then policies in place to increase economic activity need to incorporate music. These policies were not in place in New South Wales until October 2020. In London, they did not exist in 2015 when grassroots music venues were closing. And the impact of COVID-19, and how the music sector has recovered thus far, demonstrates the fragility of a "vibrant music economy" in places that lack robust links between music's needs and the needs of economic developers.

Nashville and Austin have been significantly impacted by the pandemic, like all American cities. Both grew in part due to their association with music and the interest it engendered, but neither were able to shield their music stakeholders — artists, venues and businesses — from the impact of the pandemic. This resulted in a paradox of sorts, where economic development policies that promoted music as a reason to invest were not enough to create a support structure to shield those responsible for its success.

The more attention these cities received, due in part to a thriving music scene, the more expensive they became — and less welcoming to musicians. This was not solely the fault of policymakers in Austin and Nashville, nor should these two cities be singled out. Across the United States and in other countries, it became clear that counting musicians and music businesses and ensuring that relief programmes were made available to them, like any other sector, was a challenge. This, once again, is a result of not incorporating music — and in many places the creative economy as a whole — into wider workforce, job and welfare frameworks. Sole traders, many of whom are musicians, were often excluded from relief programs. This was not a pandemic problem. The lack of understanding between music and the business of workforce or economic development is systemic. How music literally works, how it makes money and what it needs to thrive was separated from access to it.

Economic policies frequently affect music ecosystems in ways we don't expect. In St Lucia, for example, an import duty aimed at protecting local farmers from being undercut by imported fruit ended up attaching to mixing consoles and soundboards.[5] This made it prohibitively expensive to import high-quality equipment into the country and reduced the ability of studios to compete with others in the region. The policy was a catch-all, without any mention of music or entertainment. There was no intention to harm music producers, because there was no understanding that such a blunt instrument would do just that.

In the UK, a lack of understanding about how the music and creative economy earned income led to many musicians being left out of COVID-19 relief schemes. In a survey commissioned in September 2020, it was found that 64% of musicians in Britain were considering quitting the profession.[6] It's clear that a simple understanding of how musicians and creative support staff earn their keep needs further explanation in the halls of the British government. Understanding how operating as a freelance musician, or any artist for that matter works, how tax is paid and how their economic worth is valued was ignored, compared to support offered for full time, traditional employees.[7]

Here, one job — a freelance musician — is not as important as another job — a banker or a machinist. In St Lucia, the requirement of higher quality equipment to produce higher quality content was not understood in economic development policy, so the competitiveness of the product suffered. It is akin to deliberately growing smaller bananas for export, knowing full well the product would be inferior and unable to compete. But here, the priority was to ensure imported bananas and coconuts were far more expensive than those grown locally. That's all. Music and culture didn't get a look in.

Think about how this would manifest itself in most other sectors. Would we equip computer programmers with Pentium 486's and first-generation iPhones rather than modern computer equipment? Would we remove modern harvesting equipment from farmers and force them to pick all their fruit by hand? Yet these are frequently the equivalents in music policies regarding economic development. In Alabama, the state's core investment tax credit, Growing Alabama, specifically prohibits investing in culture as an economic tool.[8] This is how the gig economy — which originated in the music industry — gained steam. When traditional economic development does not incorporate music as a sector, an industry, a vocation and a product, music isn't the only sector that suffers.

Here's how to reverse this: a music expert would be hired by the organisation or local consortium responsible for economic development. A pitch deck would be developed, not only highlighting the quality of life that music can bring — venues, festivals and so on — but the business ecosystem that can support studios, production companies, riggers, songwriters, educators and others, along with music's place in marketing opportunities, both in the physical and virtual space. A music expert would be included in economic development boards and commissions to ensure music is incorporated into wider civic budget decisions. An explanation of the role of music would be made public, similar to how any other sector would be marketed to. Cross-departmental meetings would be held regularly to better understand and strategise how decisions made to attract a large employer, for example, could be enhanced by including music, or ensuring that a joined-up approach is taken when tourism campaigns begin again to attract visitors. And most importantly, a research and evidence base would be developed, mapping physical assets, measuring economic impact, surveying artists and creating policies to incorporate music into existing economic development objectives, from attracting the work-from-anywhere crowd to creating a higher-wage and skilled economy. This process — and this is what it is, a process — would be codified in the bylaws of the organisation or within city code. And a music representative, be it an officer or liaison, will be tasked with creating, maintaining and improving it.

If the blueprint is turned into action, over time there will be little fuss dedicated to music, because it will have the requisite resources to measure it. The process in Huntsville — a dedication to incorporating music into economic development policy — had been codified.

Music and Education

Alongside economic development, a key component of a successful music policy is how music is treated across education policy. Without music education, there is no music ecosystem. However, the prioritisation of STEM (science, technology, engineering and maths) over STEAM — the same but with the arts included — is another trend that demonstrates a lack of understanding of the value of music and the arts in general. Music education, in those countries and cities where it is offered, is frequently the preserve of those who can afford it or focused on specific genres of music. In the UK, A-Level (ages 16-18) music education has declined by 38% between 2010 and 2018.[9] In 2019, a poll of music teachers and schools revealed the breadth of the cuts. According to the *Guardian*:

> A poll of more than 1,000 heads, teachers, music service managers and instrumental teachers suggests that while

music education has improved in some areas, there is patchy provision nationwide. Some 97% of classroom music teachers lacked confidence in the government's handling of it. The report paints a picture of creeping cuts to music education, a demoralised workforce with poor employment conditions and huge inequality in instrumental provision, with children from families earning under £28,000 a year half as likely to learn a musical instrument as those with a family income above £48,000. And 89% of parents are making a financial contribution towards instrumental lessons.[10]

In the academic journal *Arts Education Policy Review*, four themes are outlined to explain this decline: curriculum development deprioritising music and the arts, the standardised curriculum removing music, funding being more scarce, and music advocacy on a global scale failing to successfully advocate the value the subject brought to the classroom.[11] This article highlighted cities and countries where budgets were available to support music education, but political choice supported other subjects. Traditional music education in many education systems is non-existent. In places where music education is robust, such as in China or North Korea, only specific forms of music are taught, such as Western or Eastern classical music traditions, choral singing or opera. These are valid, impactful genres, but they are not the only ones. A failure to understand the impact music education has on cognitive development, literacy, interpersonal skills and cultural education, plus limiting genres on offer in the classroom, reduces the impact a music ecosystem policy can have on the development of people and places. If kids are not being taught to experiment with, appreciate and learn instruments, then music will not play as active a role in their lives as they grow up.

If we think about music education differently, not as a standalone subject to create the next generation of professional musicians, but as a societal and cognitive development tool, much like maths and science, every community would benefit. A robust music policy framework would make this happen, as it would have the necessary data and evidence to demonstrate the return on investment such a strategy brings. There would be a cost-benefit analysis employed, but the benefit would not be restricted to music, and would instead be looked at holistically, as a necessary skill and subject to develop well-rounded, engaged minds.

This commitment would be a foundational policy in the framework: the permanent marker etched on the blueprint. Without robust music education, there is little hope that the other outcomes that music could deliver communities would be realised, including fostering a thriving commercial music economy or creating enough music to fill venues, arenas and stadiums, be it the reason fans are there or as an accompaniment to another occasion.

Moreover, the type of music that students could access, be it through a particular genre or instrument, would not be didactic. Resources would be made available so it is up to the student to choose. Instruments such as piano, guitar and stringed instruments remain at the forefront of traditional primary and secondary music education, but intentionally including drum machines, samplers, turntables and music production would be standard. This requires school boards and governing bodies to commit to developing and implementing music curriculums, and regions, provinces and nations funding them. This means tax revenue would have to be dedicated to this pursuit, which would require a robust analysis to demonstrate the return such an investment would bring. The more places committing would widen the datasets available to measure this, which would further define and defend the investment. As 2022's music education review in the UK concluded, one that committed an additional £25m to schools (a drop in the bucket, but still welcome),

> excellent music education opens opportunities, but it is not simply a means to an end: it is also an end in itself. It gives children and young people an opportunity to express themselves, to explore their creativity, to work hard at something, persevere and shine. These experiences and achievements stay with them and shape their lives.[12]

Communities that lack this provision limit the benefits, and without music education, the rest of this blueprint loses impact. There is less economic development, jobs and, as we'll see, benefits to tourism, health and wellbeing if there is no foundational and accessible music education. At the same time as increasing the investment for schools, the UK Department of Education reduced higher-education music and arts funding by £50m, with the threat that A-Level or high school music education could disappear in the nation by 2033.[13]

If a holistic approach was taken, as this blueprint dictates, music would not be left in the hands of the private sector, which often puts it out of reach of lower-income students. Budgets to bolster education frameworks in developing countries would include music, even if it is restricted to voice and choir if instruments are not available. The benefits across cognitive development, economic empowerment, community cohesion and simply creating better places to live for all of us would be measured. This would all be standard — not a nice-to-have, but a requirement. Because it would demonstrate, time and time again, fiscal and societal return on investment.

Music and Tourism

Often the most prominent way music is used in and by places is to promote them. Some places are gifted with histories and famous artists. Others benefit from a landmark venue or festival. But few comprehensively assess and understand music as a tool to promote destinations. There are significant opportunities for all communities.

Here are a number of examples of music tourism: A lone guitarist strumming Django Reinhardt in the corner during brunch. A meticulously choreographed cover show on a cruise. A music festival. Passing a street performer performing a song you recognise. Hearing a familiar song on a speaker in a taxi or at the airport. Taking a picture at a street crossing because a band walked across it 50 years ago. Returning to the scene of a music video and recreating it yourself on TikTok.

These experiences are come upon in two ways: deliberate and accidental. Travelling for the purpose of experiencing music or a music attraction, like a pilgrimage to Graceland as part of a trek across the US, finally going to Glastonbury or retracing Drake's steps from the video he shot in New Orleans or visiting Mozart's childhood home or BTS' headquarters, is a *deliberate* act of music tourism. People set out for that particular music-led experience and it is the primary justification for the trip. Stumbling upon music while experiencing a place or those who inhabit it, be it live or over a speaker, is an *accidental* form of music tourism. Both can be strategised for and optimised not only to work in tandem, but also complement other reasons people visit, spend money and experience a place, or are marketed to consider it as a place to visit. Places that deploy this blueprint would have an intentional understanding of all music assets, and map each touchpoint, recognising how heritage (what came before) and living culture (what is being created now) can be promoted. Cities and places that lack blueprints either prioritise one attraction or leave it up to chance.

Making a plan requires mapping, coordinating permitting and licensing procedures where needed, while also working with music tourism attractions and providers to weave the story of music into the wider story of the place. If a series of large-scale concerts are happening, being able to engage with accommodation providers to promote ancillary events such as afterparties requires coordination. Moreover, strategising for year-round engagement, especially in colder communities, involves understanding local music ecologies better — because these are the artists performing locally year round. When coordinated and thought-through, music makes people stay longer, listen more intently and share their experience. But often, music tourism is left to those whose business trades in it. Ticketing providers assume the role of destination marketers, so much so in some communities, such as Branson, Missouri, that ticketing agencies are permitted to open so-called "welcome centres" to entice visitors with their events whilst ignoring others.[14] A lack of joined-up thinking leaves certain experiences ignored and others oversubscribed. In some cities and places, a poorly updated listings calendar is the beginning and end of a music tourism strategy.

There is a guide to Puerto Rican music on the national tourism board website.[15] This makes sense because the success of Daddy Yankee and Luis Fonsi's hit "Despacito" in 2017 increased enquiries to visit Puerto Rico by 45%[16] — the love that listeners had from this one song nearly doubled the interest in visiting the island. This has been further capitalised on by Discover Puerto Rico, which utilised music heavily in its Have We Met Yet campaign that supported the reopening of the country after Hurricane Maria.[17]

Brand USA, the United States' destination marketing organisation, has also furthered music tourism policy. From 2019 to 2021, it used music to sell the American experience through its Hear the Music campaign. Its former VP of Integrated Marketing, Tracy Lanza, told me the impact of Hear the Music increased overall searches in visitors looking to travel in the United States, especially in the South, where Mississippi even brands itself the "birthplace of American music".[18]

Few places treat music the way Brand USA has. The more common way music is incorporated into promotion is through promoting something else, like a theme park or famous movie, or offered as something to do if there's nothing else available — that concert is happening over there at that venue, but only if you haven't found something better to do, or the movie theatre is closed.

This is made worse because music does not comfortably fit into how tourism is assessed. Music tourism is primarily a cash-in-hand business at the grassroots end and controlled by multinationals at the top, as much of it is focused on live music. The taxes that fund tourism campaigns come from hotel occupancy surcharges, and outside of large-scale events and festivals, it is difficult to measure music's role in increased occupancy. Anecdotally, large festivals and events increase occupancy, but how can we know if the jazz pianist over brunch left such an impression that a couple decided to stay an extra day to take in more of the sights? As a result, most revenue to promote destinations comes from accommodation taxes, and arguing that a portion of it be spent to invest in one's music ecosystem is difficult. Instead, a ticket levy is often the best proposition, but most of these are to support the individual venue hosting the events or the company facilitating it.

While some specific moments — such as encountering a busker on the street or a jazz pianist at brunch — may be untraceable in influencing how hotel taxes are spent, recognising, planning for and investing in tourism is knowable. This includes strategising music throughout the entire visitor experience, from arriving at an airport or a bus station and incorporating music, either via live performance or on the overhead PA (Nashville, Tulsa and Seattle do this well), to providing playlists and content for local hotels or incentives, to hosting music in restaurants, to ensuring street performance is regulated and promoted, to upselling additional events to those attending a flagship concert, to working with local artists on design and merchandising. Music tourism can be approached holistically, rather than ephemerally (a festival or event) or relying on one specific asset (a hit song, famous artist or venue) as the sole source of promotion.

According to UK Music, the only trade association that has measured music tourism independently of other sectors of the music economy, it found that "music tourists from overseas spend, on average, £910 while attending festivals and £602 while attending concerts (average tourist spend is £600)".[19] Simply, investing in music tourism alongside economic development and education makes financial sense. Music tourists spend more. That's reason enough to adopt this blueprint.

Music, Safety and Equality

Music brings people together. But it can also tear people apart. Inequities in society are represented in our music ecosystems. Societies that are structurally and systemically racist or classist have systematically racist or classist music ecosystems. How music is invested in, which music is prioritised and which is ignored, or in worse case criminalised, and who has access to music — performer or listener — is affected. In the UK and the United States, for example, while millions are invested in certain genres, drill, grime and other forms of hip-hop music have been used in court to argue a defendant's violent nature. We're talking about song lyrics here, not specific actions, in countries that protect the right to free speech.[20] In October 2022, Jamaica banned music referencing crime and drugs, ultimately restricting a vast majority of the country's popular music.[21] All this does is restrict creativity, while providing an excuse to not tackle the core problem — and the inequity that created it — in the first place.

A blueprint that does not recognise and address inequity is doomed to fray and rip. It isn't worth the paper it's written on. Inequity in music, much like in everything else, is deep, long-standing, multiplicitous, systemic and dangerous. It impacts each policy area. For example, when it comes to music education, there's an over-prioritisation of Western classical music over other forms of music in most publicly funded schools. A chronic underinvestment in music provision in lower-income communities leaves music education as a privilege only the wealthy can afford. Music deserts emerge, where access is reduced in certain areas, outside of the reach of some. This is compounded by other equity issues, such as housing insecurity, access to high-speed broadband or accessible public transportation. Moreover, if one cannot afford a computer, music becomes further restricted.

In terms of economic development, a lack of supportive tax and job-creation policies leaves those wanting to pursue a music career relying on a cash-in-hand economy, where benefits, a pension, sick or vacation leave and childcare are unavailable. Those setting up music-related businesses rarely qualify for grants and banks often refuse to lend to music businesses or artists, seeing them as risky borrowers. I have first-hand experience in this with Sound Diplomacy. As a company associated with music, we never qualified for start-up loans. Instead, we relied on an overdraft facility, which required personal guarantees — something many music entrepreneurs are unable to provide.

Society's prejudices trickle down into music in abhorrent ways. As outlined earlier, rap lyrics can still be used as character references in criminal trials, despite a new bill introduced in the US Congress to outlaw the practice, as it infringes on the right to free speech.[22] A system of policing that targets musicians and music genres from predominantly Black and Brown diasporas leads to venues being closed down simply for promoting certain genres of music, or artists being targeted for their beats, rhymes or verses. This occurred in London through a police monitoring tool called Form 696, which asked venues to report on the backgrounds and races of performers in advance of the gig. Many events were shut down due to being so-called "high risk", but it was fraught with racist and prejudicial decision-making. The process was abolished in 2017, led by the Night Czar and a number of proactive police officers. I attended several of these meetings, as it was when I was consulting with the Mayor of London in the early days of London's night time economy policy development. Unfortunately, as it is in many places, the form may have been abolished but the root causes remain, with the Metropolitan Police still being accused of racial profiling in 2023, much as they were years previous.[23]

This is also being addressed in Madison and in other communities, but accepting this as a systemic problem is being taken seriously in too few places. Recent tightening up of noise ordinances make this worse, because they disproportionately impact communities of colour. Much like everything else.[24]

Moreover, we live in a misogynistic culture that accepts that some women may never feel safe in a festival crowd. A lack of investment in access, especially physical access to venues and spaces for those with mobility issues, or investment in music and creative engagement for those with seeing, hearing or other cognitive disabilities also remains a systemic challenge. It goes on and on. Everywhere.

Music cannot solve all of these issues, but it is a far more neutral solution to assuage community inequity. In general, few of us disagree that music is, inherently, a good thing. Most of us, in one way or another, enjoy music. And making one's music equitable impacts everything, because music touches everything.

There are actions that can be incorporated into a music ecosystem blueprint from the beginning to address these issues. An anti-racism and LGBTQI+ charter with incentives, tax breaks and funding tied to those who demonstrate best practice would encourage diverse investment. We could employ sign language interpreters at concerts above a certain capacity. Mandatory anti-bias training for venue, festival and other service sector staff, as well as the police and other front-line workers who interact with them, would create more watchful ears and eyes, especially at large-scale events. Resolutions could be introduced to create a system of fair pay, no matter where someone lives. This would require, in some places, intellectual property law to be rewritten, adopted and adhered to. Exploitative secondary ticketing could be banned, as it has been in Quebec, Canada.[25] Music and creative education in the most deprived areas could be invested in, because of the return on investment, rather than just because it is the right thing to do. Those creating and maintaining music policies should also resemble the demographics of their community. Lastly, a genre-agnostic policy could be developed, so all genres have equitable access to whatever resources are available. The history of spending millions on one building for a few particular genres of music at the expense of everything else should end.

If all decisions made in enacting this blueprint were made equitable, a healthy music ecosystem would emerge. It would lead to more music tourists because there will be a more diverse offering to promote. It would support more new businesses, because confidence will grow across the community that their music, or the ideas surrounding music, matters. It would attract more talent, especially as cities and places are competing for high-skilled talent that can work from anywhere. It will expand audiences, because fewer tickets would be swooped up by resellers and exploited for three or four times the ticket value.

More music, if properly managed, is one key component that not only creates vibrant communities, but sustains them. It would create an ecosystem with skilled jobs that cannot be automated and are far less extractive. Music is a long-tail business and if more music rights are created locally, more are registered to tax-paying residents who will then earn from them. At the same time, communities that aim for high bond ratings, to increase the debt they can borrow to invest in their communities, would benefit through music's impact on increasing quality of life. Huntsville has one of America's top bond ratings.[26] It had it before we did our strategy, but it has retained it throughout and is one of the reasons why it was voted the best place to live in America. It can borrow, invest locally and pay its debt back.

Hip-hop, one genre that is part of every community, is, in and of itself, an entrepreneurial ecosystem.[27] Significant ancillary revenue can be extracted from songs across film, fashion, mixed-media, food and beverage and other sectors. Multiple skills are honed in developing and growing careers in the genre, from increasing literacy to film editing. It is inherently accessible, requiring very little start-up capital. And it is a global language that brings people together, cutting through language, race and culture. But in some communities, it is discriminated against. In others, criminalised. Worse than that, writing a lyric can be used against you in court. The sheer idiocy of not seeing this as what it is, a powerful job-creator and social development tool, beggars belief. Especially when it is the world's most popular genre, according to *Billboard*.[28]

If racism, inequity, gender bias, a lack of support across disabilities and protected characteristics or other forms of discrimination persist in the policies, practices and day-to-day activity in one's music ecosystem, any strategy written to grow it will fail. And while we cannot fix one's music ecosystem without addressing the wider inequities in how we govern, manage and extract wealth from our cities and change who benefits from it, music can be a powerful voice across wider built-environment policy, if it is built from a blueprint of anti-racism, anti-discrimination, inclusivity and fairness. Music is one of our most trusted unifiers. If it is incorporated as such into civic policy, its impact is widespread.

Music, Our Health and the Human Condition

There is a substantial body of scientific research that demonstrates the positive impact of music on our health, both physical and mental. It promotes cognitive development and positive interactions in children. It can be a tool to combat depression and anxiety and support mental health care. It is a powerful treatment for those with dementia and Alzheimer's, as it provides a "cognitive boost".[29] It is inherently a part of our workouts, running clubs and Peloton classes. It is the soundtrack to life-altering events such as weddings or funerals. It is what unites us in churches, synagogues, temples or mosques, at rallies and protests and at sporting events. It is a part of all of us.

However, measuring this value in economic terms is difficult. Can we quantify the improved wellbeing and comfort of a late-stage dementia patient in a hospice, because she has access to her favourite song from her childhood? Or can we measure the potential impact that music has in accelerating a couch-to-5k running challenge? This return on investment is much more difficult and, as a result, is the woolliest, more abstract concept to qualify and include in a music policy. But if it's not in there, and articulated properly, music will never provide the most impact possible in communities.

It is not enough to innately recognise music as a net positive to society. It requires codifying. Instead, we still leave access to music — in whatever way we come across it — as an individual pursuit without recognising that to protect this *individual* access to music, we require *collective* action — a policy. We can set benchmarks and work towards them together. Pitfalls and challenges can be unearthed and measured. Investment can be scrutinised, and one-by-one, music will become more a part of society through the policies it makes, rather than as an ad-hoc accompaniment to our lives, one of us at a time.

When classical music is played on public transit, it tends to calm those often in a stressful situation getting to work in a crowded transit system.[30] When a particular hymn is sung at church, it brings peace to those worshipping. When the call to prayer is heard, it tells entire populations to stop what they are doing, reflect and take the time to pray. The power of music, in these cases, is enormous. But without the speakers on top of the mosques or the sound systems in underground stations, none of this would be possible. Codifying, measuring and creating policies to measure the role of music on our health and the human condition would produce insights that would not only save money, but would also make places better.

The Paradox Pitfall

The main challenge to communities allocating the time, resources and expertise to creating a music ecosystem blueprint is simple. If there is no policy, or even if we go further, if there was no music education provision, no concerts, no festivals and no music in care homes, as we experienced during the COVID-19 lockdowns, *there still is music*. The lack of a music policy does not mean music disappears. Music still exists, but it is compartmentalised and not incorporated into how we govern and improve our communities. If music was a right reserved only for the wealthy, or only those from a certain race or background, *there'd still be music*. If all speakers went suddenly silent around the world, *we'd still have our voice*. Music would remain. And this is the crux of the paradox. The fact that *it can't go away* is the problem. No matter how much music education provision is cut, we can still listen to the Beatles. It doesn't matter if no more hit songs are made in Puerto Rico because we have "Despacito". And it is this false equivalence that is the ultimate challenge to overcome. What came before, what we already have access to, is seen as good enough. And this sense of things being *good enough* furthers inequity, reduces access to music and makes places worse. The assumption that music will always be there is what leads us to take it for granted, and allows for it to be governed by policies that have little to do with music and be used as a tool to further injustice.

Adopting a music ecosystem blueprint is a way to change this. This is our ultimate challenge. Without a robust music ecosystem blueprint, the infrastructure is incomplete or, in its worst case, broken. Despite data demonstrating that investing in music is a net benefit across wider economic policy, few governments take music seriously. To date, only Colombia, the Netherlands and the United States have used music as primary marketing tools on widespread tourism campaigns. The success of "Baby Shark" did not prompt a discussion that music should be included in all nursery and primary school education. "Baby Shark" was successful without a comprehensive music ecosystem policy underpinning it, so we continue to hope and assume, rather than plan.

These assumptions that music would take care of itself is how most communities engaged with it in March 2020, when the COVID-19 pandemic forced the closure of much of the live music industry. What has happened since further reinforces the opportunities that investing in music can offer. The pandemic offers substantive lessons, if we choose to heed them. And what can follow, everywhere, is a framework where music is contributing to better, more carbon-negative and equitable communities. But we need to first understand what happened, in order to chart what we need to do.

CHAPTER 6
MUSIC ECOSYSTEMS AND A PANDEMIC

I travelled a lot right before the world shut down in March 2020. I spent two weeks in the United States, visiting Denver, where we were to hold a Music Cities Convention, before travelling to Omaha to pitch for new work and New Orleans to follow up with friends. After returning to London, I then went to Abu Dhabi, to attend the United Nations' World Urban Forum, where I was giving a presentation on the role of music in meeting the United Nations' Sustainable Development Goals. In June, I was due to head to Seoul for the ninth edition of the Music Cities Convention, five years to the month that we launched the event in Brighton. Then, in September, Denver was meant to be the location for the tenth edition of the event. There were big plans for Denver. We would hold the conference at Denver's flagship arts and cultural centre, in partnership with the city's vast creative community. We'd then spend a day at the iconic Red Rocks Amphitheater before heading to Fort Collins, home to the Music District, a few square blocks outside of downtown dedicated to music development and one of the best living labs of what a thriving bricks-and-mortar music ecosystem project can be.

If there is one place that best epitomises the impact that having a blueprint and investing in music can have, it is Colorado. The state published a music strategy. It houses music and the wider creative industries within the state office of economic development. It enlisted academics and practitioners to develop the strategy and invested in its recommendations. The City of Denver also has its own music strategy. A number of initiatives were pioneered in Denver and surrounding cities, including a "starving artists policy" at fast-casual burrito restaurant chain Illegal Pete's, offering musicians a free meal, no matter who they were.[1] The Bohemian Foundation, a private not-for-profit organisation in Fort Collins, invested in the Music District, a cluster of buildings just west of downtown filled with services, educational programmes and infrastructure for supporting music education, business development and skills. Denver was home to Youth on Record, a landmark programme that hired musicians to teach in inner-city schools and operate an after-school studio and music incubator, which led to a number of student-teacher collaborations. It also operates the local festival, Underground Music Showcase. The Levitt Pavilion, a free-to-all outdoor amphitheatre, opened in 2019. The state's music strategy led to the creation of Take Note Colorado, which aimed to provide music education for every child in the state, and the Colorado Music Ambassador scheme, which began with DeVotchka's Shawn King acting as a state music supervisor, a sort of matchmaker between local bands and local businesses. Many of these initiatives were featured at Music Cities Conventions in the past, including the first one in Brighton. It was a point of pride to host the event in Denver. Colorado was not without its challenges, particularly relating to urban poverty and underinvestment in majority Black and Brown communities, but these initiatives and many more made up one of the most effective music ecosystem blueprints I knew. I shared its best practices all over the world.

For the last few years, I'd meticulously planned two- to three-week trips around the United States, becoming a travelling salesman. These trips became part of my routine. Sitting on planes for hours on end became natural. Plus, I was able to go back to Toronto and visit my family and see parts of North America few do. I learned which airport was best to be stuck in, how to weave through airports in the most efficient manner, where the best food was, what lounge felt like an escape and how to best plan connections. Each day of these trips was planned meticulously, meaning any flight delay would mess up my schedule. In January and February 2019, the trip was 37 days and 23 cities, encompassing every time zone in the United States and Canada. Once on that trip, a flight delay in Dallas meant a night at the airport.

Most city visits went the same way. I worked with local advocates to bring together people we'd need to win over — the people who had to see that investing in music meant investing in themselves. I made friends with musicians, club owners and arts workers, but also city councillors, funders, property developers and local businesspeople. In Omaha, over 30 people took time out of their day to listen to me talk about the impact a music strategy could have on their city, a place I had been to twice and knew little about. In Madison and Milwaukee, it was the same.

I explained each section of the music ecosystem blueprint and how music can be a job creator, tourism driver, a tool for equitable growth, a way to attract talent and promote a "work from anywhere" approach. I would recite the glass of water analogy — comparing the infrastructure we ignore that's required to facilitate clean tap water to explain the impact of music ecosystems on communities — in dollars and cents but also in mindset, pride of place and community development.

Once enough key people get it, the conversation changes from "who's responsible for the work" to "who pays for it". Because few cities have a music strategy budget line in their capital fund, unlocking the money takes time. It can be a conversation that lasts months. The desire to do something doesn't always mean a city will. There are places I've been speaking to for years and, despite all the will in the world, these questions remain unanswered. In most cities, such as Omaha, there's never been a successful argument made to pay to create a blueprint. At the same time, money is being spent in other ways, such as refurbishing a concert hall or to support racially diverse public art commissions. This can delay a music audit, not because the community doesn't want it, but because there are other priorities.

Why music?
Why now?
Why not other art forms?
How does this apply to our existing strategic plans?

These are the questions I answer, and spend weeks and months preparing for. Omaha was inching forward to assigning a budget for music. A dozen other cities were doing the same. It was proving to be a fruitful trip.

At the United Nations' World Urban Forum, the largest conference on sustainable urban development, I participated in two panel discussions about the value of music in the context of global development. I was speaking with people who fund large-scale development projects rather than the practitioners on the ground that I met in the United States. A trick in these conferences I use is to get everyone to sing. It breaks the ice and reminds us how unifying music can be. This is something I learned from Aubrey Preston, who joined me at the previous World Urban Forum in Kuala Lumpur. After our panel, he proceeded to get the audience to join us in a rousing rendition of "You Are My Sunshine". No matter what language you speak, everyone knows "You Are My Sunshine". "If you're going to pick a song, pick one everyone knows," he remarked. So, in Abu Dhabi, in front of 100 dignitaries, philanthropists and human rights advocates, I did the same. It didn't work as well as it had in Kuala Lumpur, but I made a few dignitaries laugh.

The conference was far quieter than the event we attended in Kuala Lumpur. One of the reasons was that the entire Asian delegation — including China, Thailand, Korea and Japan — cancelled their trip last minute due to an outbreak of the then-new coronavirus, COVID-19. There were discussions of the implication of the virus at the conference, but they were few and far between. Abu Dhabi was normal. Bars and restaurants remained packed. No one wore masks.

After four days in Abu Dhabi, I flew back to London. That was the last flight I would take until autumn 2021.

In October 2019, I was introduced to the Mayor of Kansas City, Missouri, Sylvester "Sly" James. He was coming to the end of his term and setting up a consultancy with his Chief of Staff, Joni Wickham. One minute into our first Zoom call, I loved Sly and Joni. Later, when visiting Kansas City on the American trip, Sly couldn't go ten feet without being stopped by a constituent thanking him for his work. A dozen pictures were taken with him while we watched a blues band at Knuckleheads, a local venue. A donor bought us a cocktail as we sat for dinner. We hit it off so well, we invited them to London to meet for a few days in mid-February, in between my trip to the United States and Abu Dhabi. When Sly and Joni left London, we began pursuing opportunities, which included another road trip in the United States, to include SXSW festival in Austin, Texas, and Treefort Festival in Boise, Idaho. A number of clients and leads confirmed attendance at both. At the same time, I arranged meetings for MIPIM, the world's largest property developer conference which also took place in March in Cannes, France, before the next trip to the US. 2020 started well.

Then the cancellations began.

Right after I returned from Abu Dhabi in early March, much of Europe had locked down. Two weeks previous, Sly and Joni were in London. We even went to a gig, the funk band Lettuce. It was no doubt a super-spreader event.

On my birthday, 16 March, my girlfriend and I took the afternoon off and walked to our local pub for a few pints. Then British Prime Minister and former Mayor of London Boris Johnson was on the screen, fielding the first of what was to be many shambolic press conferences. He said the UK was going into lockdown in a week, on 23 March, to combat the spread of COVID-19. Staring at the screen, it felt like we were in the bar at the end of the world. A smattering of locals, each quietly sipping their pint, were thinking that it may be their last in the pub for a while. The pub closed an hour later.

One of the Lucky Ones

I know a few people who have sadly died due to COVID-19, but compared to many others, I have been lucky. Few of my immediate family and friends have had adverse health problems because of the virus. Sound Diplomacy is not a hospitality business, so we were not forced to close. We adapted the businesses and increased our capacity to operate online, including giving up our physical offices in favour of home working, and creating virtual versions of our Music Cities Events. Our Music Cities Convention in Seoul was moved, first to September, then November, and was eventually held as a hybrid event — both virtual and in-person. Denver was cancelled. As the pandemic worsened in the United States in the spring, it did not feel right to celebrate an ecosystem that had been upended by the pandemic, even online. Our partner's focus pivoted from organising the event to deploying relief funding, which

which remained the case through 2022. Impressively, $1m was secured to support Denver's musicians and venues.[2]

In the first lockdown, music became a powerful tool to maintain interpersonal relationships when we were all stuck in our homes and flats, should we be lucky enough to have one. Uplifting stories emerged, including concerts held on balconies or choirs reconfigured so they can be coordinated online. At the same time, Live Nation's share price dropped by 34%.[3] Thousands of GoFundMe campaigns were launched to support cancelled tours, struggling promoters and artists. In the course of a few months, the arguments I used to convince people I visited in January and February to invest in their music ecosystems felt outdated. What mattered more was halting evictions, providing healthcare in overburdened hospitals, stocking food banks for those recently unemployed and organising virtual schooling. While some countries offered safety nets for their creative practitioners and businesses, these were the exception, not the norm. Most ignored artists and the creative workforce.

The impact on musicians, the live music sector and the workers that support it was significant. Austin lost an estimated $350m due to the cancellation of SXSW.[4] This is one festival, in one city. While the figure includes musicians', filmmakers' and entrepreneurs' fees to perform and the ticket revenues the festival would generate, the vast supply chain that serviced the festival was equally hurt. This included the city's hotels, some of whom take up-to 70% of their revenue in the two-week event, or the Uber and Lyft drivers, equipment providers, food carts, street cleaners, bartenders and private healthcare providers. SXSW is, at its core, a music festival. But economically, SXSW is a festival that uses music to create economic benefit for Austin and the wider region. The city as a whole is poorer without it. This is the same with all festivals. Coachella Festival in Indio, California, brought an estimated $700m to the region in 2017.[5] This includes the spend at hotels, bars, restaurants, Airbnbs, Uber/Lyft, parking charges, sales tax and tips. This income disappeared in 2020, as Coachella was cancelled. There are tens of thousands of Coachellas, large and small, all over the world.

Every music venue closed its doors. Some were able to sell archived recordings, merchandise or takeaway food and later act as vaccine distribution or immunisation centres, but for the most part, in the first phase of the pandemic, the music sector was in freefall, with core costs mounting and little or no revenue coming in. In some countries, relief programs were instituted to support independent businesses, but the complex nature of these premises' workforce created holes in the support. In the UK, while the furlough scheme covered 80% of an employee's salary up to £2,500 a month, it did not apply across the board to freelancers (some did qualify for self-employed income support, but many creatives did not qualify) or contract employees, which make up a significant portion of music venue workers. Sole traders were left out. Small independent venues may only employ two or three people full-time; the rest are freelancers or directors of their own limited companies, each of whom faced barriers to accept support. A security guard may be an independent contractor, for example, and marketing services be outsourced to a freelancer. With a venue going dark, income dries up across the supply chain. At the same time, utility costs, rent, equipment rental and other fixed costs kept coming. Most artists faced the same dilemma; incomes derived from a few different jobs, rather than being a single, salaried employee. Often those jobs were in hospitality or tourism, two of the most affected sectors. Cruise ships not sailing left many musicians without a revenue source. Tour cancellations impacted not just artists, but lighting designers, riggers, drivers, caterers, tour managers and other support staff. Nowhere was this more pronounced than in the United States, where little to no relief was made available to independent venues and music businesses in the first lockdown.

As the days and weeks passed, these challenges took a toll on venue owners. Steven Severin from Neumos, a venue in Seattle, was interviewed bi-weekly in *Billboard* magazine. The interviews chronicle the problems he faced keeping his venue afloat, and the toll that took on his mental health. On 12 May 2020, he reflected on the loss of another venue, Re-Bar:

> There is a venue that has been in Seattle for 30 years called the Re-Bar and they called it over the weekend. It just sucks. They've been around for 30 years and they aren't going to open again. Nirvana did their *Nevermind* release party there. It does everything. They had the longest-running house DJ night in the country called Flammable. It's been running for over 15 years every Sunday. Dina Martina owned it for some time so there were a lot of drag shows. They were an important part of the community, and they are done. They may open up in a couple of years in a different space, but you can't recreate the magic. And they are friends of ours. We're all sitting here thinking the exact same thing could happen to us.[6]

On 20 August 2020, he said:

> If somebody doesn't step up, we go away. That's how it works. Hopefully, the federal government steps up. We keep hoping and wishing, and nothing is happening. More places are going to go down while waiting. And people are losing more money trying to stick it out longer. At some point, everyone has to make that choice of whether they think they are going to get saved or they just keep throwing money out the window.[7]

On 13 November 2020, after Joe Biden's presidential win was confirmed, Severin reflected:

> I slept almost 30 hours over the weekend. I was so tired. We knew we had Biden. We knew we made it through the election. It was just... letting that stress go and trying to get it out of my body. It is still there. I am still getting it out of my body. I was surprised how much [the election] did affect me and everybody. It was so rad to see people kind of floating a bit. What a difference.[8]

In this interview, Severin thought that concerts would return in full force in the third quarter of 2021. Neumos is one of thousands of small- to medium-sized businesses where the nature of their work — how it operated, was staffed, paid its bills and what impact it had on its community — was not well understood by the bureaucratic systems and structures aimed at supporting small companies. In the United States and many other countries, running a music venue was seen as a pursuit of passion, not a job-creator, job-retainer, community development tool and talent incubator. This is not a mindset that COVID-19 created. It is as old as the live music industry itself, the original gig economy.

While Seattle, Washington and King County had policies and infrastructure to manage and support their music ecosystems, they weren't enough to respond to the challenges thrown up by the pandemic. But their response was far better than most places because there were individuals in place to respond. Most other places were not in such a position.

This is not specifically a music issue, but few overarching issues that impact the development and success of music ecosystems are solely *music issues*. The live music sector was exposed as fragile. Particularly for those who perform in small rooms, at weddings or in cover bands, it is a cash-in-hand business. You arrive, perform or support a performance in one way or another, get paid and leave. As a result, adding up the economic value of such a business was more difficult than an organisation with a set number of salaried employees or a product that was being manufactured with a supply chain that could be tracked and monitored. Artists might do well on merchandise one night and less so on another. If a lighting engineer couldn't make one show, another would be called to fill in. Some music was better for takings at the bar, while other concerts were loss leaders, either to support emerging artists or other community events, like an open-mic night. Operating a grassroots music venue or working as a freelance artist or support worker in the sector is both a pride of passion and a set of calculated risks. If you do enough of it — play enough shows, stage enough bands — a medium will emerge that equates to a bottom line, and an income.

This fluctuation in time, revenue and personnel is hard to track in the manner in which traditional business is tracked. This is the gig economy, and prior to COVID it functioned well enough for many to choose to work within it. It provided freedom, so long as there were enough gigs to go around. When all gigs stopped, the lack of foundation to support this work was laid bare. Local live music ecosystems could not bear the weight of all the cancellations. Livelihoods were lost in two or three months.

In its mid-year statistics in June 2020, the Recording Industry Association of America (RIAA) revealed that revenues for its members — multinational major labels and publishers — increased 5.6% in the first six months of 2020.[9] The value of streaming grew 12% during that time, a stat echoed six months later in a report by the RIAA's British counterpart, the British Phonographic Industry (BPI), which reported an 8.2% growth in music usage in

2020.[10] By the end of 2021, global calculations showed an 18.5% growth in the total value of the global recorded music market.[11] At the same time, over 70% of the value of the live music sector was wiped off the map, most of it without means to access insurance or backpay. But as the lockdown wore on, the amount of music consumption increased, and with it the revenues of the global companies that dominate the sector. Universal Music Group generated $1bn in revenue from streaming alone in three months in 2020.[12] While artists that relied on live income and the ecosystem that supported them suffered, the commercial rights-led music industry thrived. The more we stayed at home, the more music we listened to, and the more record labels benefitted. And interest in music rights, especially from hedge funds and venture capitalist firms grew. Blackstone, KKR and others began to invest in music rights, seeing that increased consumption meant consistent revenue. In 2021 alone, over $5bn was invested in music rights, leaving *Bloomberg* to call music a lucrative alternative asset class.

What was made clear as the pandemic continued was that there is no singular "music industry". If certain sectors are thriving, such as trading existing music publishing rights, it does not mean the entire music ecosystem is. Local economies continued to experience profound contraction in both 2020 and 2021, even with relief funds eventually being made available to support their recovery. A guitarist who could count on a wedding per week before the pandemic did not benefit from Fleetwood Mac or Neil Young selling their rights to a hedge fund.[13]

Listening During the Pandemic

There are three roles in the commercial music industry — those who make it, those who trade and disseminate it, and those who consume it. Since the reproduction of sheet music and the emergence of the first copyright management society, SACEM, in France in 1851, the revenue from copyrighted musical works has been split between the artist, the disseminator (in most cases a record label) and the publisher. Before that, most music was commissioned and agreements were transactional, a sort of pre-gig economy where the artist or composer was paid for their time but did not receive royalties. After 1851, the right to reproduce the music — both the musical work itself and the reproduction of it — was due a fee. When music was reproduced onto a recorded format, the agreements were simpler. Artists were paid a fee as an advance to record, given tour support, and then once the advance was recouped, a split was agreed. As revenues declined with the reduction in physical sales, so did tour support and the size of advances offered to artists. When streaming emerged, a new revenue model was struck that offered artists and songwriters a new source of income for their work but did not represent, for a large share of recorded artists, a fair revenue split. As artist Nile Rodgers explained in the United Kingdom's Department of Culture, Media and Sport's enquiry into streaming: "50% of the streams of a Spotify user goes to record labels, 30% stays at the platform and less than 20% goes to the performers."[14] More music being listened to at any one time is positive. The more music in our ears, the more musicians are being paid — so the story goes. The reality is far more complex. While streaming revenues increased because more of us were at home and had no choice but to listen to music via Spotify, Apple Music or Pandora, the rate of return for our favourite artists differed widely, depending on who they are, where they are from and what their recording contract dictated, should they have one. Artists may have been receiving hundreds of thousands of streams, but in some cases, that equates to the same net revenue as a hoodie at a gig or a few concert tickets. Most artists were not able to replace their live income with the income they received from streaming. So we listened to more music, but those responsible for it were not the main beneficiaries. The middlemen, as most of them remain men, were instead.

This highlighted the problem of many communities' approach to investing in their local talent and emerging music infrastructure — they end up leaving it to multinational corporations. Being able to upload one's music on Spotify, for example, creates the myth that access leads to revenue and success — even if every local independent venue closed, local music was still available via global platforms, and there were now more to choose from. If a local artists' work is available to everyone, everywhere, through a major streaming platform, this is surely good and, taken at face value, an opportunity to succeed. At the same time, multiple other revenue-generating opportunities emerged, or became better known, while we were all stuck at home. Some artists began earning revenue through Twitch, the Amazon-owned gaming platform, or through independent virtual concerts, or through expanding their Patreon offers. The number of platforms that offered an opportunity for artists to generate revenue increased. What did not increase, however, was the time to maximise one's offer on their platforms or educational access to learn how to best use them. School boards did not suddenly add how to monetize one's music on Twitch as part of a high school music curriculum, and those who now had to replace income from live music were, in essence, starting from scratch online. Some succeeded, as some always do, so we migrated online.

These success stories, however, only reinforced a longstanding truth that is enhanced through investing in local music ecosystems. If you have fans, they will support you. Melissa Etheridge's "Concerts from Home" series is one such example. According to her manager Deb Klein in an interview with *Pollstar*:

> Her daily free live streams between 16 March and 12 May totalled more than 7.3 million views, with 74,480 shares. In June 2020, Etheridge TV has had an average of 1,000 monthly subscribers per month at $50, along with selling a couple of thousand single tickets per month for $10.[15]

Klein continued:

> We had been working on a paid model before this happened; we realised the pandemic wasn't going anywhere soon. And Melissa tours quite a lot, seven months out of the year, she's never had a summer off, this past summer was the first time. And so early on we were looking at what she was going to do. And one thing that's really important is her relationship with her fans, performing — the way it makes her feel, the way it makes them feel. It's a very symbiotic, two-way street when artists are doing live concerts. And every live show is different because every live audience is different. There's different energy and there's an exchange. And so I was [questioning] what are we going to do? How can we recreate this?[16]

There were many other examples. Curbside concerts using the back of flatbed trucks were crisscrossing their way across Canada, the US and Australia. One such act, Tall Heights, toured backyards, gardens and public squares, working out socially distanced events with hosts in advance and selling as many tickets a particular place could accommodate. They made each available via a weekly live stream, *Tall Heights Thursday*. In a *Medium* post, the band revealed they earned "$11,000 from ticket sales and $6,500 from merchandise".

They added: "Making that much money in the middle of a pandemic was game-changing, not only for our short term financial security but because we now know there's a path forward."[17]

However, for every Melissa Etheridge or Tall Heights, there are thousands of studio, session or bar musicians who earn their living on cruise ships, weddings or playing on songs without you knowing they are there, whose income did not move from the stage to the livestream. By February 2021, a *New York Times* article stated that New York alone had lost two-thirds of its creative workforce, many of them musicians who left due to lack of affordability and job prospects.[18] This is one city, in one country. The impact for most was devastating.

Most local and touring musicians, without national insurance, pension contributions, healthcare or other services offered to full-time workers, lived in an ecosystem where the existence of the next gig meant they were able to survive. What the pandemic showed is that music as an artform and those responsible for its production should be seen as separate entities, and one need not exist for the other to succeed. We can have music without musicians now, so long as there were musicians then. This revealed an incredible opportunity, should communities seize it. Music consumption — and with it the amount of money it made — grew during the lockdown. It became something that surely we didn't need to live, but clearly could not live without. It was also clear that if an emotional connection was made between an artist and their listeners, the listeners would continue to invest in and support them.

However, while opportunities remained for many artists to connect with their fans and earn a living, most did not have that privilege. And the support net was full of holes, if it had been stitched together at all. What was needed was to redraw and implement a new blueprint after lockdown.

What was emerging, in real-time, was the best case ever for showing, in detail, the value that music ecosystems bring to their communities and how a lack of investment, care and effective policymaking makes all places worse. This was an opportunity to demonstrate how and why having a music ecosystem policy is crucial. The act of placing the same level of importance on music as any other public good was on display, be it on a livestream, an Italian balcony or a choir on Zoom.

At the same time, the music industry organised itself in better ways than I had ever experienced in my two decades working in the sector. The commercial music industry is a bruising, competitive and unforgiving business. Collaboration is prevalent, but self-interest is the guiding principle. This changed a little in 2021, through new trade associations such as the National Independent Venue Association (NIVA) in the United States and LIVE in the UK. Before the pandemic, the live sector avoided engaging with the government, because it usually created conflict, either about regulation or tax. This is because most communities lacked a music ecosystem blueprint, so most often engagement came when something went wrong, such as a noise complaint or a protracted permitting negotiation. Proactive evidence-making and lobbying began, changing the adversarial tone into one aimed at demonstrating the value of live music, and with it the need to support it in freefall. Relief programs, insurance for venues and festivals coming out of the pandemic and other concessions emerged, because lobbies existed to fight for them in a unified manner, rather than for self-serving policies. This further highlighted the challenges, because there was a trade association to do so cogently, with one voice. A lack of any music ecosystem policies in most communities made problems worse. Musicians and other workers were not classed properly in employment codes or venues were unable to apply for tax relief, for example. But leadership emerged to lobby to fix these problems, and this collective action was replicated around the world, and in many places it worked. Governments were beginning to listen. Music ecosystem policy, it seemed, had never been more important.

The first lockdown was in effect a living lab for music ecosystem policy. It was a constant, real-time reminder of what was wrong and how it could be fixed. On display was a world that needed music, but was mired in inequality and those who were most responsible for creating music were treated with disregard. We were all consuming clean water, but the aquifer was being depleted. Now was the time to advocate for this shift, a global rethinking of music ecosystem policy.

Looking Back, Many Lockdowns In

In the United States, $15bn of funding for cultural venues was approved in the second stimulus package, offering a lifeline to independent music venues, movie theatres and other cultural establishments.[19] Festivals began announcing line-ups for 2021, hopeful that vaccine distribution and widespread testing would ensure the event could take place safely and with enough tickets available to be profitable. This, as we learned, was not to be the case, as a further wave cancelled a majority of festivals for the second straight year, including SXSW, which was held online. Others were cancelled due to adverse weather, like Bonnaroo, further showing the mammoth challenge climate change is accelerating, in addition to COVID. In countries less stringent with their restrictions, such as the UK, festivals happened, including Reading and Leeds. In the Netherlands, tens of thousands of nightlife advocates staged protests called Unmute, similar to the SLAM rally, beaten down by continued lockdowns.[20]

Over three years since the first lockdown was announced in mid-March 2020, much can be learned from this collective experience. First, the response to the pandemic further revealed vast, widespread and systemic inequality across music and cultural ecosystems. This was reflected in overall societal inequalities, intentional state policies that supported some more than others, and a belief — or wilful ignorance — in many places that music was not worth supporting. From the onset, the music industry — especially those representing the live sector — were placed into a narrative that victimised the business and the workers within it at no fault of their own. This is not because of the business itself, but because in many places, music was not considered to be "business". It was entertainment, and that was a luxury when there is a public health emergency. Without structured guidance governing capacity, social distancing and other safety parameters all being measured in real-time and adopted in wild variation, there was no ability to offer simple, clear advice or recognise the impact of closures on those who work in the sector. When your business is predicated on people congregating in enclosed spaces, many of them inefficiently ventilated basements or buildings built for another purpose, it was clear from March 2020 onwards that business as usual was untenable.

The message became frighteningly clear: working in the music ecosystem was a privilege, not a right. It was not a core business that required investment. These were not frontline workers. There was no urgency to protect their jobs. Instead, music was seen as a recreational activity that would only be eligible for relief after the *important industries* were taken care of. The vast supply network that pays their bills and mortgages by servicing live events, from tent rental firms to haulage companies, caterers or security firms, were not linked to the survival of live music. However, these skills of staging events and building temporary infrastructure supported other needs, such as establishing field hospitals, morgues or vaccine centres, proving the transferability of these skills that had been honed in the music ecosystem.[21] Jobs in the music ecosystem were deemed less important, less professional and less urgent than other sectors, such as manufacturing, fishing or oil and gas, for example. While no government policy outrightly stated this (bar a few ill-conceived mishaps), the lack of support for freelancers, sole proprietors and contract workers was evident en-masse. This is the standard narrative. I experienced it when I pursued a career in music. It's fun, you should be *so lucky doing something you love. What a privilege.*

Add to that, for those getting rich off the value of music rights, the fact there's little incentive to change, which can further disassociate the economic upside of music with the need to invest in it in communities for that upswing to be maximised. For example, the Michigan Teachers Pension Fund owns a stake in Concord Music, a large independent label, publisher and administrator; it does not mean that music education in Michigan is better protected and invested in, despite the fact that doing so would increase the chances of the investment performing well.[22] Music is being used to fund teachers' retirements in the same place that music education is not available to all kids across the state.

The ubiquity of music during the pandemic shows how important it is. We now have a once-in-a-generation opportunity to improve policies for everyone. If the music ecosystem functions as a local luxury underpinned by global systems that make it ubiquitous and, as a result, create a veil of permanence, it fosters inequity. As it is conceived by many, the simple act of making music available is what matters more than investing in the music ecosystem. And this is why we are missing out on building these ecosystems that create a circular, thriving economy, placing music at the heart of local community and economic development. COVID-19 has revealed this faster than any of us could have imagined. The pandemic has changed the role of music in cities and urban settlements. But this change can be for the better.

So Let's Grasp This Opportunity

We must recognise the impacts of the virus are not unique and will likely happen again, whether it's the closure of events and venues, the cancellation of festivals or global challenges to supply chains. We must recognise that climate change will irrevocably impact our towns, cities and places, and with it the music and entertainment economies that reside within them. Adverse weather is cancelling more gigs than ever before, and this will increase. Building resilience or the ability to withstand shocks and wear and tear is as important in our music ecosystems as it is in our water, electricity and healthcare infrastructures. A sudden shock can cost far more than yearly maintenance. In order to plan for these crises better, we must all accept what is worth planning for and what is accepted to be left to chance. So far, the music ecosystem has been left, in most cases, to chance.

In some countries, healthcare is a human and moral right, so a percentage of tax revenue is allocated to supporting it, so it benefits everyone. In places that offer universal healthcare, it is there whenever it's needed, free at the point of use — but what if it were suddenly taken away? Equally, we often only think about clean water or electricity as important when they're not available. While regulations vary wildly, there is a broad understanding of the importance of these resources and a need to invest in providing them for as many of us as possible. Three of the 17 United Nations' Sustainable Development Goals are predicated on clean air and water, and the other 14 can't function without it. We accept that purifying water and air costs money. So does lighting and heating homes. So we plan, invest and pay for it, often at great expense.

If we value music and culture in the same way as we value healthcare, clean air and water, then we have to treat it similarly. The pandemic has shown that access to music and listening to it is important. How it gets to us and who made it, and how they are treated in the ecosystem they inhabit, is unfortunately nearly always seen as less important.

The pandemic has laid bare the lack of planning and understanding how music works in cities, and what is needed so it can be optimised, and in doing so, enhance everything around it. Few studies have explored the value that music therapy can provide for those suffering from mental health illnesses, and the potential savings investing in such treatment can provide versus prescribing costly medication. There have been few cost-benefit analyses of the outcomes of students who have access to music as they grow versus those that do not. Little analysis has been conducted to understand the value of a thriving music venue or record store and the pull it has to change and improve the neighbourhood around it. We value festivals and heritage, but often only when it is being experienced. Few communities have taken time to simplify and better organise their permitting framework, so it saves time and money, but also enhances accountability.

There are exceptions, as I have outlined in Melbourne, London and elsewhere, but these are just that — exceptions. In most other places, there is a series of missed opportunities, and with it, money being left on the table. Investing in one particular genre, venue or festival does not cut it. Leaving all aspects of the music ecosystem to the free market won't either. And none of this would matter if the pandemic revealed that, in fact, music was not important, not integral, not needed. If music consumption reduced and interest in music declined, especially when one of the primary means of consumption — going to see it live — was eliminated, then there'd be no need to argue for greater investment and a greater system of care to support music-makers, businesses and all those who listen to, enjoy and internalise their content.

The pandemic was the ultimate stress test, and if music didn't pass the test, then my point would have been disproved. But the opposite occurred. And when COVID-19 becomes part of our collective memory, which it will at some point, will we have learned to prepare better for the next crisis, be it climate change, a natural disaster or a future pandemic? Will we develop more robust policies to support music ecosystems? Will music ecosystem investment become a part of cities', regions' and nations' capital budgets, so it is, like a film office, a line on a spreadsheet? Will cities invest in offices of music and nightlife and the expertise required to run them equitably? Will governments that lack infrastructure to support copyright realize the errors of their ways and take steps to correct it? Will more people realise that access to music is not a right, but a privilege, and that privilege can only be sustained by remunerating those responsible for it fairly? Will those who see music solely as entertainment change their tune, so to speak, and view music as any other industry — one that has winners, losers and is as serious a job as anything else? Will the next kid who dreams of being a professional musician be encouraged by their parents, or be told to go and get a real job? Will we, as a society, decide to pay more for music and ensure that the bulk of that investment goes to artists, songwriters and musicians first, rather than multinational corporations? Will an aspiring musician in a developing country be able to realise their ambition as much as a musician from a more developed country? Will the colour of one's skin always be a variable that determines access, opportunity and outcomes? Will cities and places take the time and invest resources in research, measuring, adding up and understanding their music economies' and ecologies' strengths and weaknesses? And when we face our next crises, will those who know how to access support be the ones that benefit the most? Will banks recognise the value of music-related ideas and provide financing, much like any other sector? And will we, as neighbours and communities, recognise the value of music rights, or will we leave that investment and reward to Wall Street? Will we change, or will the fight continue? I don't know. But I remain hopeful.

When I am able to visit cities and pitch again, I will speak about music differently. I will ask why festivals and venues were able to trade if they didn't have the insurance provisions available to them so that they would be protected in all eventualities. I will ask why a city couldn't create its own online framework to bring together and promote and showcase local music. I will enquire why, in order to increase tax revenue and protect IP, a city would look to invest in music rights, much like it invests in other local infrastructure, through its public sector pension funds or other investment pots, providing capital in the present, while like any other investor, building a potentially valuable portfolio for the future that all community members could benefit from. I will ask why a music policy hasn't been adopted, if those living in the city enjoy listening to music. I will explore the economic value and cost-benefit that a group healthcare plan for musicians could have and see how, through partnering with larger city-wide provisions, it could be created in places without universal cover. I will ask why all music-related businesses, from all communities, weren't mapped and assessed before the pandemic, so it would be easier to find them when a crisis hit. I would like to know if there are prejudices in how certain genres are funded, which leads to some being lavishly supported while others are ignored and, in some places, criminalised. I will enquire if music — as a policy area — is contributing to structural racism. But, and most importantly, I won't demand any answers to these questions. Instead, I will seek a willingness to join me, or whoever they choose, in seeking these answers out. And with it, a better, more resilient community. One that treats music seriously, for each and every resident.

In answering these questions, we can rewire every community's music ecosystem. We can use the blueprint, at the same time recognising that what works for some may not work for all. The pandemic revealed how powerful music is. It can be worth so much more, in so many ways. It can be a powerful tool in recovery, but it's also invaluable for reimagining what localism, community and quality of life actually mean. We have to act for all, not just for some. It is time to introduce this new normal. And whatever that may be, it must be better than what existed prior to any of us knowing the word "COVID-19".

EPILOGUE
THE WAY THINGS COULD BE

The Future Music Ecosystem

An aspiring twenty-three-year-old guitarist is on her way to perform at her local venue. She's confident about her performance, having learned music since nursery school. Since the age of eleven, she's used VR software that allowed her to jam with other kids from around the world online. She has also learned to play the kora, having been taught by a friend in the Democratic Republic of Congo that she's never met. At her gig, she will debut a song she's written on it. Through her social media feed, she communicated the show across the city, and via a fingerprint scanner on everyone's smartphone, tickets have sold out. And for those who missed out, she's not worried. If someone doesn't make the show, her app will text them for the automatic personal live stream. Wherever they are, her fans can immerse themselves through VR, with the payment automatically split between her, her supporting musicians, record label, publisher and management company. She's also happy to know that she's being paid fairly, since the government mandated equal pay for women in 2024. Fans of all ages can attend the venue as facial recognition at the bar knows who is of legal drinking age, and treats them accordingly.

The last time she played live, it was outdoors in a local park. A benefit concert. The stage was inlaid into the park with speakers built into the ground, removing any need for her to bring bulky backline. The speakers generate electricity while she plays, which powers the lights and broadband infrastructure in the park. The cups given to the attendees are biodegradable and have seeds built into the sides, so even if they're left on the ground, they do no harm. Because the park already has a built-in backline, she saved money getting to the gig, which is important as she played for free.

Unfortunately, on her second song, the sound engineer accidentally turned the sound up too high. How did she know that? Sensors installed throughout the park monitored the noise levels, providing real-time reports to local authorities who alerted the promoter that it was reaching neighbours. A ping registered through her ear implant, confirming the breach. The app then pinged the soundboard, and the level was automatically lowered, triggered through the sensor. And the quality never altered, on stage or off. The audience had no idea.

Music isn't her full-time job, at least not yet. She's studying to become an urban planner, specialising in culture. In 2024, many universities launched cultural and music planning degrees, as cities around the world were rewriting their cultural infrastructure and strategic growth plans. There's a rush to qualify planners, as over 100 cities in the world are eagerly trying to map their cultural infrastructure and get in line with international standards. The best cities, she hears, are updating their plans every two years.

She read an article last week about a planner who created a tool to build inexpensive sunken stages under grasslands, powered by solar energy and capable of lighting the public realm within 300m of the stage. These stages are noise neutral, VR compatible, and receive planning permission in the detailed design phase, so performing legally on them is automatically allowed. Performance slots are booked and managed through an app. The permitting process is automatic. The infrastructure also recycles water and composts waste.

The app has been wildly successful. A recent study in London shows a 100% increase in live music in 2028, and not a single noise complaint lodged related to music since 2026.

Satellite-enabled, renewable 6G WIFI made it easy to start and maintain a band, something she continued despite her coursework increasing. While her bandmates opted to study at different schools, high-speed eco-trains allow them to meet weekly, and because four hundred studios and rehearsal spaces were developed underneath train stations and railway arches across the UK since 2024, rehearsing has never been easier or more convenient. Like venues, every studio is zero-waste, carbon-neutral and self-sufficient. The entire music industry is now carbon neutral. Streaming is generating energy that's being sold back to the grid. Bandcamp and Deezer's listeners are powering her favourite studio in north London.

If she can't make practice for some reason, she can still participate at home through the inexpensive VR home-kit she bought in 2028. Thanks to the co-working and artists' spaces next door, she's met a prospective designer for her album artwork, and a stylist to help with live performance.

Since 2026, noise complaints in houses and flats have been reduced twenty-fold following the introduction of mandatory insulation and triple-glazing of homes in entertainment districts. The Agent of Change principle getting ratified by over 190 countries at the United Nations' General Assembly in 2025 helped, making it a pillar of sustainable urban development. At the same time, cases of dementia — a disease her grandmother had ten years ago — have reduced after a cause of the disease was discovered in 2024. Music became part of the course of medication to treat it, among other interventions. Thankfully, those studying music therapy have tripled, with half a dozen new programmes in the UK alone since 2024.

Her smartphone — now containing the keys to her home, ID, facial scanner and banking details — offers unlimited streaming where she pays a fair rate, linked to inflation, for access to the music. Her digital "paper trail" shows exactly who got paid for each nano-second she streamed, and if she wishes to digitally top-up payments for artists she's particularly interested in, she can. This was made permanent through the UN's declaration in 2025 that access to music and culture is a basic human right, and as such, consumption of it must recognise and remunerate those that created it fairly and transparently. This is helping musicians in developing countries, she hears, who are paid automatically when their music is streamed on YouTube, directly to their mobile phone. Her kora teacher was able to increase his instrument collection, for example.

After the gig, she walks home. Many of the new apartment blocks she passes now have a cultural use, be it a community centre, day-care, day theatre or music venue on the ground floor and basement. She passes a busker playing some Bob Dylan. Great music never disappears. Using her fingerprint, she gives him a few pounds through a sensor embedded in the pavement. She gets home, closes the door and enjoys the silence, despite her neighbour having a house concert next door. Her new-build, completed in 2026, features state-of-the-art noise-cancelling insulation.

Tomorrow, she has a meeting with her town's Head of Music to discuss a future festival performance. From 2024, every city, town and region around the world set up a music office to start treating music and culture the same way they treat schools, hospitals and other necessary pieces of infrastructure. She needs a permit for the future performance. She's filled out the form online and, as a previously registered applicant, has gone through facial recognition and is a trusted supplier. As usual, she must sign and abide by the zero-waste, zero-emissions mandate the global music industry agreed to.

The next day she plans to head back to the rehearsal space, which is filled with 6G WIFI and big screens for linking performers around the world in real-time. She wants to write another song. But this time, with a Chinese mouth harp melody she learned from a friend in Chengdu. Maybe she'll go for dinner with her partner afterwards. Nights off are few and far between.

Notes

Chapter 1: For Something to Exist, It Must Have a Policy

1 https://musicvenuetrust.com/wp-content/uploads/2016/09/Defining-Grassrots-Music-Venues.pdf

2 https://www.prnewswire.com/in/news-releases/copenhagen-named-monocle-magazine-s-best-city-in-its-2021-quality-of-life-survey-886938304.html

3 https://monocle.com/film/affairs/most-liveable-city-2019-zurich/

4 https://www.swissinfo.ch/eng/clean-water-for-all_a-look-inside-zurich-s-water-treatment-system/43833918

5 https://nights-2022.org/

6 https://variety.com/2019/music/news/long-may-they-run-podcast-phish-history-1203336394/

7 https://www.usatoday.com/story/life/music/2018/01/03/rap-overtakes-rock-most-popular-genre-among-music-fans-heres-why/990873001/

8 https://urbanization.yale.edu/about

9 https://trademark.trademarkia.com/nashville-music-city-85442022.html

10 https://americanhistory.si.edu/blog/nashville-music

11 Havighurst, Craig. *Air Castle of the South, The Making of Music City*. University of Illinois Press, 2007, XVIII.

12 https://www.nashvillepublicradio.org/post/curious-nashville-why-were-music-city-according-ken-burns

13 https://trademarks.justia.com/770/53/nashville-music-77053856.html

14 https://www.rollingstone.com/music/music-country/historic-
    rca-studio-a-saved-from-demolition-183201/

15 https://s3.amazonaws.com/nashvillechamber.com/PDFs/
    MusicStudy_2020_Dec16.pdf

16 https://www.nashvillesmls.com/blog/did-you-know82-people-
    move-to-nashville-every-day.html

17 https://www.tennessean.com/story/entertainment/
    music/2020/09/02/nashville-music-venues-cares-act-aid/
    5693766002/

18 https://www.nashville.gov/sites/default/files/2022-01/COVID-
    19-Financial-Oversight-ARP-Funding-Overview-Music-Venues-
    Study.pdf

19 https://savingplaces.org/places/nashvilles-music-row/updates

20 https://www.nashville.gov/Codes-Administration/Property-
    Standards/Code-Enforcement/Zoning-Code-.aspx

21 https://www.mnps.org/strategicplan

22 https://www.thrillist.com/entertainment/nashville/nashvilles-
    hip-hop-scene-underground-music

23 https://www.washingtonpost.com/arts-entertainment/2020
    /06/09/country-music-george-floyd-reaction/

24 https://www.rollingstone.com/music/music-country/nashville-
    music-row-historic-place-endangered-842067/

25 https://www.kut.org/post/origin-austin-live-music-capital-
    world-take-two

26 https://www.sxsw.com/about/history/#timeline

27 https://www.kvue.com/article/money/economy/boomtown/
    study-austin-is-third-fastest-growing-city-in-us/269-
    d857070c-52be-4a91-b331-06fcb13e1ccd

28 https://www.planetizen.com/news/2021/12/115566-austin-
    musicians-squeezed-housing-crisis

29 https://www.austintexas.gov/page/creative-space-assistance-
    program#:~:text=The%20Creative%20Space%20Assistance%
    20Program,funding%20for%20creative%20space%20purchases.

30 https://www.austinchronicle.com/music/2022-05-27/faster-

than-sound-the-austin-music-census-returns-while-the-live-music-fund-faces-delays/

31 https://eu.statesman.com/story/news/politics/county/2019/09/20/austin-city-council-dedicates-36-million-in-annual-hotel-taxes-to-live-music/2731293007/

32 https://www.austintexas.gov/news/reopening-guidance-austin-music-venues-released-support-COVID-19-recovery-planning

33 https://www.texasmonthly.com/the-daily-post/eight-things-we-learned-about-austins-music-industry-from-the-austin-music-census/

34 https://www.npr.org/sections/therecord/2017/02/24/516904340/the-struggles-of-austins-music-scene-mirror-a-widened-world?t=1567165174785

35 https://www.statesman.com/news/20190328/survey-austin-tech-industry-grew-by-5200-jobs-in-2018

36 https://www.statesman.com/news/20181213/apple-plans-new-1-billion-austin-campus-5000-more-jobs

37 https://communityimpact.com/austin/northwest-austin/city-county/2018/12/14/williamson-county-pursuing-15-year-incentive-deal-for-new-apple-campus-in-austin/

38 https://www.statesman.com/news/20190926/austin-incomes-rise-yet-again-while-poverty-rate-sees-surprising-uptick

39 https://www.kut.org/post/study-says-austin-has-lowest-levels-income-inequality-among-large-us-cities

40 https://communityimpact.com/austin/economic-development/2019/02/28/report-austins-economic-growth-is-leaving-black-and-latino-communities-behind/

41 https://www.austinchronicle.com/daily/music/2020-09-17/music-workers-rally-for-dedicated-city-funding/

42 Cowan, Cody, Austin Music Policy Recommendation, 15.05.2020.

43 https://liveforlivemusic.com/news/oregon-venues-relief-funds/

44 http://50statesofmusic.com/state/oregon/

45 https://www.austintexas.gov/sites/default/files/files/EGRSO/
    TXP-Austin-Music-Impact-Update-2016-Final.pdf

46 https://www.numbeo.com/cost-of-living/compare_cities.
    jsp?country1=Austria&city1=Salzburg&country2=Austria
    &city2=Graz

47 https://www.brookings.edu/research/lost-art-measuring-
    COVID-19s-devastating-impact-on-americas-creative-
    economy/

48 https://www.mmtimes.com/news/myanmar-support-film-
    music-industry-amid-COVID-19.html

49 https://www.theothernashvillesociety.com/

Chapter 2: Music Ecosystems for All?

1   https://www.heraldsun.com.au/news/victoria/melbournes-
    180th-birthday-how-carlton-collingwood-fitzroy-have-
    changed/news-story/000d607751a6372def10ac54f919690c

2   https://www.theage.com.au/entertainment/music/melbourne-
    music-icon-the-tote-shuts-up-shop-20100115-ge88dr.html

3   https://www.smh.com.au/politics/federal/the-tote-a-case-of-
    liquor-licensing-downing-one-too-many-20100118-mgqe.html

4   https://www.heraldsun.com.au/news/law-order/scourge-
    of-violence-spreads-from-melbournes-cbd/news-story/
    dc457c9474f53459c77c86562a534bc7

5   Interview with author, 24 Nov 2019

6   Baker, Andrea. 2018. *The Great Music City*. Palgrave MacMillan;
    London, pg. 180.

7   Ibid.

8   https://www.abc.net.au/news/2018-04-12/melbourne-is-the-
    live-music-capital-of-the-world-census-shows/9643684

9   https://www.mirror.co.uk/news/uk-news/families-complain-
    noisy-neighbours-every-22179154

10 Baker, Andrea. *The Great Music City*, pg. 181.

11 https://www.abc.net.au/news/2019-09-08/sydney-lockout-
    laws-rolled-back/11489806

12 https://www.bocsar.nsw.gov.au/Pages/bocsar_pages/Alcohol_
    Related_Violence.aspx
13 https://au.finance.yahoo.com/news/16-billion-thats-much-
    sydneys-lock-laws-cost-citys-economy-053457918.html
14 https://www.timeout.com/sydney/nightlife/meet-michael-
    rodrigues-the-man-whose-dream-job-is-being-sydneys-night-
    mayor
15 https://www.london.gov.uk/sites/default/files/londons_
    grassroots_music_venues_-_rescue_plan_-_october_2015.pdf
16 https://www.reuters.com/article/us-usa-music-cities/when-
    the-musics-over-cities-suffer-as-venues-fall-to-developers-
    idUSKCN1LX24D
17 https://nowtoronto.com/music/features/vanishing-music-
    venues-a-progress-report/
18 https://www.vancourier.com/news/dwindling-rehearsal-space-
    has-vancouver-musicians-in-a-jam-1.21557819
19 https://money.cnn.com/2010/02/02/news/companies/
    napster_music_industry/
20 https://www.cbsnews.com/news/after-napster-the-music-
    industry-winds-up-humming/
21 https://www.bbc.com/news/entertainment-arts-60837880
22 https://www.ifpi.org/ifpi-global-music-report-global-recorded-
    music-revenues-grew-18-5-in-2021/
23 https://variety.com/2020/music/news/riaa-recorded-music-
    revenues-1234765304/
24 https://tarzaneconomics.com/undercurrents/copyright-2001
    -2020
25 https://www.theguardian.com/music/2018/oct/05/10-years-
    of-spotify-should-we-celebrate-or-despair
26 https://www.theguardian.com/music/2022/oct/02/no-
    tune-no-words-no-dancing-why-white-noise-is-the-music-
    industrys-newest-hit
27 https://www.marketingcharts.com/industries/media-and-
    entertainment-81082

28 https://www.forbes.com/sites/hughmcintyre/2017/11/09/americans-are-spending-more-time-listening-to-music-than-ever-before/#147752242f7f

29 https://ent.qq.com/a/20190117/008027.htm

30 https://www.nbcnews.com/business/business-news/concert-sales-are-reaching-record-levels-despite-surging-delta-variant-n1275899

31 https://www.weforum.org/agenda/2019/01/the-experience-economy-is-booming-but-it-must-benefit-everyone/

32 https://www.forbes.com/sites/hughmcintyre/2017/03/11/ed-sheeran-controls-9-out-of-the-top-10-spots-in-the-u-k/

33 https://www.ukmusic.org/news/uk-music-calls-on-chancellor-for-budget-review-of-business-rates

34 https://completemusicupdate.com/article/music-venue-trust-welcomes-50-business-rates-cut-for-small-music-venues/

35 https://www.gigwise.com/news/101355/glastonbury-pyramid-stage-performers-average-age

36 https://www.theguardian.com/music/2022/jun/24/cream-teas-rocknroll-older-revellers-glastonbury

37 https://www.rollingstone.com/pro/news/top-1-percent-streaming-1055005/

38 https://www.linkedin.com/pulse/new-year-idea-post-pandemic-lessons-from-those-who-were-will-page/

Chapter 3: Lessons from the Stage

1 https://trademarks.justia.com/770/53/nashville-music-77053856.html

2 http://www-news.uchicago.edu/releases/08/pdf/080122.music.pdf

3 https://www.lex18.com/news/wet-vote-to-bring-new-business-in-rowan-county

4 https://247wallst.com/special-report/2019/12/12/states-that-still-have-dry-counties

5 https://dunstan.org.au/wp-content/uploads/2018/03/TIR_2013_Elbourne_Report_Reverb.pdf, page 113

6 https://www.dunstan.org.au/wp-content/uploads/2018/03/
   TIR_2013_Elbourne_Report_Reverb.pdf, page 12.

7 https://www.timeout.com/london/music/boris-johnson-on-
   buskers-bagpipes-and-bob-marley

8 https://www.upsetmagazine.com/news/boris-johnson-backs-
   frank-turner-supported-campaign-to-save-music-venues

9 https://www.independent.co.uk/arts-entertainment/music/
   news/music-industry-wont-find-stars-of-tomorrow-without-
   radical-action-to-stop-venue-closures-says-report-a6700336.
   html

10 https://www.theguardian.com/artanddesign/2020/jul/24/
   our-slum-future-the-planning-shakeup-set-to-blight-british-
   housing

11 https://www.bbc.co.uk/news/uk-england-london-25642151

12 https://www.reddit.com/r/madisonwi/comments/5uj2pd/
   task_force_would_address_equity_in_madisons_music/

13 https://www.cityofmadison.com/CityHall/legislative
   Information/roster/504010.cfm

14 https://static1.squarespace.com/static/58f7f35e9f745630b
   6952af8/t/5ee8ddebfb9c756767df9120/1592319470180/
   TFEME_report.pdf

15 Ibid, page 11.

16 https://www.overture.org/about/history

17 https://datausa.io/profile/geo/madison-wi/

18 https://static1.squarespace.com/static/58f7f35e9f745630b
   6952af8/t/5ee8ddebfb9c756767df9120/1592319470180/
   TFEME_report.pdf

19 https://www.cityofmadison.com/news/greater-madison-
   music-city-receives-50000-our-town-grant-from-national-
   endowment-for-the-arts

20 https://www.tonemadison.com/articles/city-budget-proposes-
   studies-of-madison-musics-economics-equity-problems

21 https://www.tonemadison.com/articles/music-makes-money-
   in-madison-but-not-enough-for-musicians

22 https://www.tonemadison.com/articles/music-makes-money-in-madison-but-not-enough-for-musicians

23 https://www.nme.com/en_au/news/music/nsw-remove-development-regulations-on-live-music-venues-in-new-reforms-2816599

24 https://www.theguardian.com/culture/2020/nov/18/the-changes-really-are-monumental-live-music-industry-celebrates-huge-overhaul-of-nsw-laws

Chapter 4: Huntsville

1   https://bhamnow.com/2022/05/26/birmingham-is-now-alabamas-3rd-largest-city-surpassed-by-huntsville-and-montgomery/

2   https://www.al.com/news/2020/08/mazda-toyota-increases-investment-at-huntsville-plant-by-830-million.html

3   https://www.huntsvilleal.gov/huntsville-scores-dual-triple-a-credit-rating-for-the-12th-straight-year

4   https://creativeindustriesnews.com/2021/12/frances-cnm-will-spend-e194-1m-in-2022-to-support-the-recovery-of-the-music-sector/

5   https://www.al.com/life-and-culture/erry-2018/10/a64025bc636662/initial-findings-of-huntsville.html

6   https://www.huntsvilleal.gov/government/mayors-office/mayors-initiatives/music-initiative/music-audit/

7   https://www.al.com/news/2018/07/historic_florence_building_tur.html

8   https://www.waff.com/story/38801454/stricklin-hotel-in-florence-sues-city-flobama-over-loud-noise/

9   http://quadcitiesdaily.com/?p=562397

10 https://gov.texas.gov/music/page/music-friendly-communities

11 https://www.rollingstone.com/music/music-country/orion-amphitheater-huntsville-alabama-brittany-howard-drive-by-truckers-1354616/

12 https://gardenandgun.com/articles/coming-soon-huntsvilles-new-amphitheater/

13 https://www.al.com/life/2022/05/orion-amphitheater-what-it-was-like-at-alabama-venues-big-opening-night.html

14 https://www.al.com/life/2022/02/downtown-huntsville-bar-and-venue-gets-new-name-reopening-this-summer.html

15 https://www.waaytv.com/news/first-waltz-at-huntsvilles-new-orion-amphitheater-considered-major-success/article_704cefdc-d553-11ec-b546-8fbdddbb31a3.html

16 https://www.wsj.com/articles/first-came-the-urban-transplants-now-come-the-concerts-11658664001

17 https://ne-np.facebook.com/huntsvillecity/videos/huntsville-city-council-meeting-september-23-2021to-read-facebooks-community-sta/4603518056338522/

18 https://www.musicbusinessworldwide.com/ben-lovetts-tvg-hospitality-raises-50m-from-investors-including-irving-azoff-coran-capshaw-and-ryan-tedder1/

19 https://www.rollingstone.com/music/music-features/huntsville-alabama-orion-amphitheater-1234580158/

20 https://www.huntsvilleal.gov/first-of-its-kind-city-of-huntsville-seeks-full-time-music-officer/

21 https://www.al.com/news/huntsville/2021/07/city-of-huntsville-hiring-music-officer-with-salary-up-to-89211.html

22 https://www.al.com/news/2021/07/heres-what-little-richards-grave-marker-in-alabama-looks-like.html

23 https://huntsvillebusinessjournal.com/lead/2021/02/22/huntsville-music-initiative-a-duet-in-economy-and-song/

24 https://www.al.com/news/huntsville/2022/07/huntsville-music-officer-whats-his-job-what-isnt-his-job.html

25 https://www.waff.com/story/10756923/shoals-music-festival-has-huge-economic-impact/

26 https://www.al.com/life/2022/04/muscle-shoals-music-new-record-labels-filmtv-projects-on-the-way.html

27 https://www.billboard.com/business/business-news/muscle-shoals-recording-studio-region-offering-music-incentives-1235106774/

28 https://www.insider.com/huntsville-alabama-what-its-like-living-there-best-us-city-2022-6

Chapter 5: The Blueprint

1   https://www.cieh.org/news/press-releases/2022/noise-complaints-increased-by-over-50-during-first-lockdown-year-in-england/
2   https://www.offbeat.com/noise-ordinance-on-the-table-again/
3   https://www.wwltv.com/article/entertainment/outdoor-entertainment-to-be-legalized-in-new-orleans-after-unanimous-vote/289-8d87ead4-e76d-4cb4-9ed4-e0766da67aa7
4   https://www.wipo.int/wipo_magazine/en/2015/05/article_0009.html
5   https://exportsaintlucia.org/saint-lucia-music-industry-export-strategy-takes-shape/
6   https://www.classicfm.com/music-news/coronavirus/musicians-leaving-industry-encore-survey/
7   https://www.nme.com/features/excluded-choir-one-more-day-rishi-sunak-2746402
8   https://revenue.alabama.gov/tax-incentives/major-tax-incentives/growing-alabama-credit/
9   https://onlinelibrary.wiley.com/doi/full/10.1111/chso.12386
10 https://www.theguardian.com/education/2019/apr/02/school-music-cuts-inequality-demoralised-teachers
11 https://www.tandfonline.com/doi/full/10.1080/10632913.2015.1007406
12 https://assets.publishing.service.gov.uk/government/uploads/system/uploads/attachment_data/file/1086619/The_Power_of_Music_to_Change_Lives.pdf, page 2.
13 https://djmag.com/news/level-music-education-could-disappear-2033-due-lack-access-and-funding
14 https://www.news-leader.com/story/news/local/ozarks/2020/08/27/london-firm-reveals-findings-months-long-branson-theater-study/5643965002/

15 https://www.discoverpuertorico.com/article/guide-to-music-puerto-rico

16 https://explore.traveloka.com/features/despacito-boosts-puerto-rico-tourism

17 https://www.billboard.com/articles/columns/latin/8510991/puerto-rico-music-post-maria

18 Personal interview, November 14 2020.

19 https://www.ukmusic.org/news/value-of-music-tourism-to-the-uk-economy-revealed

20 https://www.dummymag.com/news/uk-drill-music-increasingly-being-used-as-evidence-in-court/

21 https://monocle.com/radio/shows/the-foreign-desk/explainer-338

22 https://variety.com/2022/music/news/rap-lyrics-crimimal-evidence-congress-bill-legislation-1235327683/

23 https://www.theguardian.com/music/2023/apr/21/theyre-doing-this-by-stealth-how-the-met-police-continues-to-target-black-music

24 https://www.wpr.org/can-you-hear-segregation-and-intolerance

25 https://www.ticketnews.com/2012/06/stringent-quebec-ticket-resale-law-goes-into-effect/

26 https://www.huntsvilleal.gov/huntsville-scores-dual-triple-a-credit-rating-for-the-12th-straight-year/

27 https://www.kauffman.org/currents/hip-hop-entrepreneurship/

28 https://www.billboard.com/music/music-news/billboard-explains-rb-hip-hop-biggest-genre-9613422/

29 https://www.cbc.ca/news/health/alzheimers-music-memories-brain-scanning-1.4895791

30 https://www.independent.co.uk/arts-entertainment/classical/news/play-classical-music-in-hospitals-and-railway-stations-to-calm-public-report-says-9732479.html

Chapter 6: Music Ecosystems and a Pandemic

1   https://www.illegalpetes.com/starving-artists/
2   https://www.artsandvenuesdenver.com/news/detail/
    independent-music-venues-and-denver-artists-receive-1-
    million-in-cares-act-funding
3   https://www.statista.com/statistics/1104240/live-nation-
    share-price/
4   https://www.sxsw.com/2020-event-update/
5   https://www.finance101.com/coachella-festival-transformed-
    valleys-economy/
6   https://assets.billboard.com/articles/business/touring
    /9376610/neumos-seattle-coronavirus-pandemic-independent
    -venue
7   https://www.billboard.com/articles/business/9437651/
    neumos-seattle-coronavirus-pandemic-hopefully-the-federal-
    government-steps-up/
8   https://www.billboard.com/articles/business/9482283/
    neumos-seattle-in-pandemic-third-quarter-2021-we-could-do-
    shows-again/
9   https://www.riaa.com/wp-content/uploads/2020/09/Mid-
    Year-2020-RIAA-Revenue-Statistics.pdf
10 https://musically.com/2021/01/04/bpi-reveals-8-2-rise-in-
    uks-music-consumption-in-2020/
11 https://www.ifpi.org/ifpi-global-music-report-global-recorded-
    music-revenues-grew-18-5-in-2021/
12 https://www.musicbusinessworldwide.com/universal-music-
    group-just-generated-over-a-billion-dollars-from-streaming-in-
    a-single-quarter-during-a-global-pandemic/
13 https://www.rollingstone.com/music/music-news/fleetwood-
    mac-christine-mcvie-catalog-rights-hipgnosis-1209306/
14 https://routenote.com/blog/record-labels-keep-half-of-all-
    profits-from-music-streaming-and-nile-rodgers-is-calling-for-
    clarity/
15 https://www.pollstar.com/article/qs-with-primary-wave-

talent-managements-deb-klein-on-melissa-etheridge-mastering-2020s-livestreaming-puzzle-147014

16 Ibid.

17 https://tallheightsmusic.medium.com/our-band-found-a-way-to-tour-during-the-pandemic-7a90acb865aa

18 https://news.artnet.com/art-world/66-percent-loss-nyc-arts-entertainment-1946971

19 https://www.rollingstone.com/music/music-features/live-music-save-our-stages-relief-1107081/

20 https://www.beatportal.com/news/unmute-protest-netherlands-joris-voorn/

21 https://www.wsj.com/articles/music-industry-offers-up-venues-for-covid-19-vaccinations-11611673340

22 https://www.pionline.com/article/20190429/PRINT/190429867/michigan-retirement-likes-the-sound-of-its-concord-music-stake

ACKNOWLEDGEMENTS

I would like to thank my incredible editors, Carl Neville and Josh Turner. This book wouldn't be what it is without them. In addition to them, there are a number of people, from editing first drafts to fact-checking and encouraging me, to who I owe my gratitude. James Drury, Helen Marcou AM, Dennis Madsen, Mark Davyd, Lohan Presencer, Jim Lockridge, Martin Elbourne, Rob Hain, Duncan McKie, Patrick Donovan, Jeff Syracuse, Montana Agne-Studier, Charlie Brotherstone, Richard Florida, Alan Davey, Dwight Ireland, Sly James Robert Horsfall, Aaron Bethune and Sandra Perens, thank you.

I want to thank the team at Sound Diplomacy, Music Cities Events, the Center for Music Ecosystems and Unison Rights, who continue to inspire me everyday. I also want to recognise that there are countless examples and initiatives that I have not chronicled in this book that deserve to be celebrated. You all know who you are.

Most importantly, this book is dedicated to my partner Alice. Without her, I would have not had the encouragement or confidence to write. And finally, to my sister Alli, who while not with us anymore, instilled the love affair I have with music that grows every day. This book is for you.

ABOUT THE AUTHOR

Photo credit: James Drury

SHAIN SHAPIRO is the recognized global expert in understanding how music and cities intersect. He founded Sound Diplomacy, the world's leading economic consultancy working with cities, governments and the private sector on cultural, leisure, hospitality and entertainment policy, strategy and creative infrastructure. Shain also leads the nonprofit Center for Music Ecosystems, which commissions research to help solve local, national and international challenges using music as a tool. He lives in London.

REPEATER BOOKS

is dedicated to the creation of a new reality. The landscape of twenty-first-century arts and letters is faded and inert, riven by fashionable cynicism, egotistical self-reference and a nostalgia for the recent past. Repeater intends to add its voice to those movements that wish to enter history and assert control over its currents, gathering together scattered and isolated voices with those who have already called for an escape from Capitalist Realism. Our desire is to publish in every sphere and genre, combining vigorous dissent and a pragmatic willingness to succeed where messianic abstraction and quiescent co-option have stalled: abstention is not an option: we are alive and we don't agree.